Albatros Aces
of World War 1

SERIES EDITOR: TONY HOLMES

OSPREY AIRCRAFT OF THE ACES • 32

Albatros Aces of World War 1

Norman Franks

OSPREY
AVIATION

Front cover
The mercurial Werner Voss first saw fighter action with *Jasta* 2 Boelcke from late 1916 through to May 1917. During this period he achieved 28 victories, despite being away from the front during April – a time during which the Royal Flying Corps (RFC) lost its greatest number of aeroplanes. Whilst with *Jasta* Boelcke, Voss flew this distinctively marked Albatros D III, which boasted a red heart insignia on its fuselage sides and top decking and a laurel wreathed swastika good luck symbol. Finally, its white nose and tail, together with two broad white bands on the upper wing surfaces, made this a distinctive machine, despite the application of standard green and brown camouflage on its wing surfaces (mauve and green was yet to come into vogue). Iain Wyllie's painting depicts the action fought over the Western Front on 9 May 1917 by Voss and 2Lt George Hadrill of No 54 Sqn, who was flying a Sopwith Pup. The latter pilot lost out in this engagement, being forced down behind German lines and captured. Hadrill represented Voss's 27th victory, the destruction of the Pup being the second of three kills claimed by the ace in this, his final day of action with *Jasta* 2. He would add 20 more victories before being killed in combat four months later

Back cover
Otto Hartmann was the leader of *Jasta* 28w in 1917. He had scored seven victories by the time he fell in combat to the guns of a No 48 Sqn Bristol Fighter on 3 September 1917

Title page spread
Seventeen-kill ace Ltn R Walter Böning flew this blue and white dia-mond-marked Albatros D Va whilst with *Jasta* 76b in the spring of 1918. However, the pilot perched on the cockpit rim in this photograph is an unknown NCO. It is possible that the latter individual took over this machine (5765/17?) after Böning was wounded whilst flying it on 30 May 1918. Note the black vertical band bordering the diamond mark-ings. The coat of arms is that of the city of Würzburg, in Bavaria, and consisted of a red and yellow quar-tered square
(*P Grosz via G VanWyngarden*)

First published in Great Britain in 2000
by Osprey Publishing, Elms Court, Chapel Way, Botley, Oxford, OX2 9LP

© 2000 Osprey Publishing

ISBN 1 85532 960 3

Edited by Tony Holmes
Page design by TT Designs, T & B Truscott
Cover Artwork by Iain Wyllie
Aircraft Profiles by Harry Dempsey
Scale Drawings by Mark Styling

Origination by Grasmere Digital Imaging, Leeds, UK
Printed through Bookbuilders, Hong Kong

99 00 01 02 03   10 9 8 7 6 5 4 3 2 1

EDITOR'S NOTE
To make this best-selling series as authoritative as possible, the editor would be extremely interested in hearing from any individual who may have relevant photographs, documentation or first-hand experiences relating to the elite pilots, and their aircraft, of the various theatres of war. Any material used will be fully credited to its original source. Please write to Tony Holmes at 10 Prospect Road, Sevenoaks, Kent, TN13 3UA, Great Britain, or by e-mail at: tony.holmes@osprey-jets.freeserve.co.uk

For a catalogue of all titles published by Osprey Military, Aviation and Automotive please write to:

Osprey Direct UK, P.O. Box 140, Wellingborough, Northants NN8 4ZA, UK
E-mail: **info@ospreydirect.co.uk**

Osprey Direct USA, P.O. Box 130, Sterling Heights, MI 48311-0130, USA
E-mail: **info@ospreydirectusa.com**

Or visit us at **www.ospreypublishing.com**

CONTENTS

WESTERN FRONT

It often comes as a shock to those starting to read about early aviation for the first time that many of the pioneering designs were monoplanes and not biplanes. This was also true of the early years of World War 1, with several successful machines boasting just one wing. The most notable on the German side was the Fokker *Eindecker* ('one wing').

The *Eindeckers* enjoyed much success in 1915-16, despite only being available in comparatively small numbers. Air fighting was just developing, and the pilots who flew these early fighters had to learn the skills. In these early days the few *Eindeckers* that arrived at the front were attached to two-seater *Abteilung* formations to act as escorts, and in between performing this primary duty, they could be used to chase Allied two-seaters away from the battlefields.

It was because there were so few of these fighters that the Germans got into the habit of defending their territory, rather than pursuing the doctrine being used by the Royal Flying Corps (RFC) – to take the war to the enemy. The RFC's policy became one of aggression through offensive action, with aircraft flying over the trenches to seek out enemy aeroplanes, and targets, inside German-held territory.

For practically the whole of the war, the German force was inferior in aircraft numbers in comparison with the Allies, which resulted in them remaining steadfastly defensive right through to the end of the conflict. Although having less aircraft overall, the Germans were not always outnumbered in the air – far from it, for their *Jagdgeschwader* and *Jagdgruppe* systems, which were adopted later in the war, could easily overwhelm the opposition in individual actions.

Once the single-seat fighters were established into individual fighting units, this became a definite tactic. Fighting on their side of the frontlines meant that German pilots could engage or disengage far easier than the British or French airmen, and if forced to come down, they were more often than not landing in their own territory, whereas their opponents, if they came down and were not killed, became prisoners of war.

THE JASTAS

These fighting units, known as *Jagdstaffeln*, were introduced in the summer of 1916. Ostensibly, they were in part the brainchild of Oswald Boel-

Albatros D IIs of *Kampstaffel* 11, KG 2, in late 1916/early 1917. Even at this early stage aircraft are adorned with white personal markings on the fuselage. The fighter third from left is Karl Schäfer's machine (D.1724/16), with his white circle emblem (*P Grosz via G VanWyngarden*)

Schäfer's Albatros D II, D.1724/16 with his personal white circle emblem. Standard wing camouflage at this point in the war consisted of dark and light green and a reddish (chestnut) brown, with blue undersides. The plywood fuselage (often left in natural varnish which gave it a yellowish look) is probably stained here with a reddish brown colour. All metal cowling panels and wheel covers were almost certainly painted grey (*via G Van Wyngarden*)

cke, a successful *Eindecker* pilot who had achieved 19 combat victories by the early summer of 1916. Taken out of combat, he was sent abroad, but returned to France with the idea of grouping the *Eindeckers* together into dedicated fighter units to be used as offensive and defensive groups. Taken up by the *Chef des Feldflugwesens,* Oberst Hermann von der Lieth-Thomsen, he ordered the first *Jagdstaffeln* into existence on 10 August 1916, having no doubt seen the logic of Boelcke's ideas, along with other input from field commanders.

By the time his idea became reality the day of the *Eindecker* was past, for the nimble scout that had caused havoc amongst Allied airmen had finally been defeated by better British and French biplanes, ushering in a new era in aerial warfare. Seeing the writing on the wall, German manufacturers had also developed several single-seat biplanes to supersede the Fokker monoplane, with the most promising designs coming from the factories of Halberstadt, Fokker, LFG Roland and Albatros.

Of these, the Albatros D I became the best known, although the Halberstadt D II and D III, Fokker D series and LFG Roland D II all saw frontline service – the 'D' stood for *Doppledecker*, or two wings. Apart from the rotary-engined Fokker D II and D III, the remaining aircraft all used in-line engines, which helped the designer to build a more streamlined machine. Indeed, the Albatros design was exceptionally 'clean', although it did have radiators on both sides of the fuselage mid-way between the nose and the cockpit. These were discarded in later models.

Whilst the D I and D II were not as manoeuvrable as either the French Nieuport Scout or British Airco DH 2 'pusher' which had combined to defeat the *Eindecker*, their speed in attack gave them the ability to both engage and, just as importantly, break off combat if necessary. The early Albatros fuselage was slab-sided, but still comparatively streamlined, although it later became rounded with the arrival of the D V in the summer of 1917.

The first Albatros machines to see frontline service were those issued to *Kampfstaffeln* (*Kastas*) attached to *Kampfgeschwaderen* (KGs). Similar to the *Eindecker Keks*, the *Kastas'* primary job was to provide bomber protection, as well as undertake occasional patrols. Pilots were often drawn from the more aggressive members of the KGs, who volunteered to fly the single-seaters. A good many future aces cut their combat teeth in these units, and although few enemy aircraft were brought down, the experience gained by these individuals would eventually prove to be very important.

Kasta machines often carried individual pilot markings, it being found desirable for pilots to quickly identify one another in the air. Rudimentary camouflage was used, which made it necessary for the national marking – the iron cross – to be painted onto a white background. Some of the early white markings had the square corners 'cut off', giving the impression to Allied airmen that the cross was on a white circle.

The first dozen *Jagdstaffeln* (*Jastas*, as they became known) were formed in August and September 1916, with a further 12 being created in October and November. Their establishment coincided with the arrival of the new Albatros and Halberstadt D-type fighters, as well as the Fokker D-type. Initially, a mixture of scouting types was often used in each *Jasta*, although it was the Albatros which eventually became the standard fighter by the end of the year. Indeed, by December 1916 the Fokker D I had been withdrawn from combat following the death of several pilots due to in-flight structural failures.

In the early war years German pilots who came directly into fighters were rare, for almost all had first gone through periods flying with two-seater *abteilung* units. This is not in itself strange, for in the beginning all German units flew multi-seat aircraft. However, once the fighting *Jastas* had been established, it became general policy that all fighter pilots had to have served for some period in a two-seater unit. This gave them vital experience not only of battle conditions, but of what it was like to be engaged whilst in a two-seater. Unlike his British counterpart, who arrived at the front fresh from completing his flying training, the German *Jagdflieger* was therefore more likely to survive his first encounters, having already got to know what the air war was like.

The make up of each *Jasta* was much smaller in overall size than a RFC squadron or a French *escadrille*. Sometimes, the pilot strength consisted of no more than eight or nine men, with perhaps the same number of aeroplanes. This also led to the continuance of the overall defensive role of the *Jastas*, despite RFC and French units generally appearing over German lines in a flight strength of five, which was often reduced to four or three through engine problems.

The tactics developed by men such as Boelcke during the late summer and autumn of 1916 centred on *Jastas* waiting until frontline observers had telephoned to say that an Allied formation had crossed, or was about to cross, the German lines, or that an Allied Corps machine was over the front directing artillery fire. Most *Jastas* had their bases close to the frontline, so it took only a few minutes for the pilots to gain height and intercept the enemy. Once they had sighted the hostile machines, the *staffel* leader would determine the best form of attack, which he would lead if he felt he had the advantage.

The prevailing wind direction of west to east helped the *Jasta* pilots in that it generally blew the Allied aeroplanes into German-held territory and then hindered them as they flew back. This gave the *Jagdflieger* a distinct advantage when these conditions applied, and of course they could break off combat at will if the going got too tough, spinning away and landing in their own territory.

All *Jastas* were lead by a *Staffelführer* when aloft, and he generally had first 'crack' at an opponent during an attack, being covered and supported by his pilots. If the attack was upon a formation of hostile aircraft, the other pilots would only enter the fray once battle had been joined. In the case of an attack upon a single opponent such as an artillery flyer, the leader would continue to fire his guns until they either failed or ran out of ammunition. Alternatively, the attack would pass to one of his pilots if the *Staffelführer* himself was hit by the allied observer, or he lost the advantage of position to another *Jasta* member.

It was in this way that many of the early German aces added constantly to their scores, and it can be seen in some *Jasta* records that often only one or two pilots scored regularly, while others made few or no claims. The latter men flew on the same missions, but it was the 'stars' that did the scoring. Of course, these 'stars' were 'good operators', who had shown themselves able to survive in combat. They were undoubtedly spurred on by the awards and honours on offer from their superiors for the completion of successful combats.

The arrival of the Albatros helped these up-and-coming aces, and it was a machine that was to see frontline combat on all fronts, but especially the Western Front, for the rest of the war – almost wholly in 1917, and in significant numbers throughout 1918.

ARMAMENT

From the start the firepower for the Albatros Scouts was provided by two 7.92 mm LMG 08/15 Spandau machine guns, synchronised to fire through the airscrew's two wooden blades. It gave the German pilots the ability to deliver a considerable 'punch' at a time when Allied aeroplanes only carried one synchronised gun, which was occasionally supplemented by a wing-mounted Lewis gun.

THE ACES

German aviation units were mostly Prussian-manned, but others were formed with allegiances to various states. Thus, *Jagdstaffeln* with a small 's', 'w' or 'b' stood for Saxon, Württemburg or Bavarian units respectively, although they were not all necessarily manned by men from those states, just as pilots from these same states were not prevented from serving in Royal Prussian units. Generally, however, their commanders had to be from the state indicated. The first 15 *Jagdstaffeln* were all Prussian.

Jasta 1 never achieved the fame one might have thought from its place and number, although it did achieve some notable successes in its early period. In all its fighting days, it only produced nine pilots who scored more than five victories – five has become the yardstick for an ace, although in World War 1 ten was the more accepted number for the Germans. A number of other aces flew with *Jasta* 1, although they scored most of their kills in other *staffels*.

Jasta 1's Hans von Keudell eventually flew Albatros Scouts after Fokker D Is and Halberstadt D IIIs. He gained his 12th victory as leader of Jasta 27 on 15 February 1917, just before he fell in combat in Albatros D III D.2017/16

Jasta 1's first ace was Kurt Wintgens, who had earlier been a successful Fokker *Eindecker* pilot. When he became part of the unit, he brought with him 13 victories, and during September 1916 his skill and prowess shone through to the tune of six more victories, before he was himself shot down in flames by French ace Alfred Hertaux of *Escadrille* N3 on 25 September.

Wintgens had all the trappings of a hero, having been awarded the *Pour le Mérite* (also known as the *Blue Max*, this was Germany's highest military honour in World War 1), Royal Hohenzollern House Order, the Bavarian Military Merit Order 4th Class with Swords and the Saxon Albert Order, Knight 2nd Class with Swords. At the time of his death he ranked only second to the great Oswald Boelcke in terms of victories scored.

The most successful of this unit's pilots was Ltn Hans von Keudell, who achieved 11 victories between August 1916 and January 1917. Having previously flown bombers and then Fokkers, he also enjoyed successes with Fokker D Is, Halberstadt D IIIs and Albatros D IIs whilst with *Jasta* 1. Promoted to command *Jasta* 27 on 5 February 1917, von Keudell had scored just one victory with his new unit when he was shot down and killed in Albatros D III 2017/16 near Vlammertinghe by a British Nieuport 12 crew from No 46 Sqn.

Vfw Paul Bona achieved all six of his victories with *Jasta* 1 between December 1916 and May 1917, his efforts to increase his tally being interrupted after his first claim due to a combat wound. It was permanently interrupted on 6 June 1917, Bona's D III losing its wings whilst chasing an Allied machine over Allemont. He was killed in the crash. Unfortunately for his colleagues, this incident was not isolated to Bona's mount, for the sesquiplane D III had an unnerving habit of suffering structural failure in flight, resulting in the death or serious injury of a number of German pilots.

Another successful *Jasta* 1 pilot was Ofz Wilhelm Cymera, who had the distinction of being shot down by British ace Albert Ball on 22 August 1916 whilst serving as a bomber pilot. Surviving this, he began to exact his revenge as a single-seater pilot with *Jasta* 1 before the year was out. Cymera achieved five victories, including No 11 Sqn ace John Quested, whom he forced down inside British lines on 27 December 1916, and the CO of No 60 Sqn, Maj E P Graves, whom he shot down and killed on 6 March 1917 – coincidentally, the major was flying one of Albert Ball's old Nieuport 17s, A213. Cymera was himself killed in combat on 9 May 1917, possibly falling victim to French ace Adjutant Lucien Jailler of N15 (his ninth of 12 kills).

Oblt Hans Kummetz commanded *Jasta* 1 from November 1916 through to September 1917, achieving six victories during this time. After a break as an instructor, he returned to his command, which by November had moved to the Italian Front. He gained one more confirmed kill before falling in combat with Camels from No 45 Sqn on 11 January 1918.

Another successful *Jasta* 1 pilot was Ltn Herbert Schröder, who gained five victories between March and October 1917. He too had been a two-seater pilot prior to joining the unit, and in November moved to *Jasta* 17, but failed to add to his score before being wounded in May 1918.

These aircraft were some of the first Albatros D Is delivered to *Jasta* 2 in September 1916. A number of the fighters have already been marked with pilot initials for individual recognition. The aircraft second from right is D. 434/16 (*G VanWyngarden collection*)

Jasta 1 claimed over 138 victories, 107 being confirmed. The bulk of these were scored on the Western Front, the unit claiming just ten kills on the Italian Front between November 1917 and early February 1918.

JASTA 2

Oswald Boelcke was given command of *Jasta* 2, and also given almost total *carte blanche* on the choice of pilots for the new unit. Not least amongst his early charges

The great Oswald Boelcke, father of the *Jastas* and leader of *Jasta* 2 in the autumn of 1916. He was killed in a collision on 28 October 1916

were embryo air fighters such as Manfred von Richthofen, Erwin Böhme, Max von Möller, Hans Imelmann and Otto Höhne. While *Jasta* 2 now had most of its complement of pilots, the unit had few aircraft, starting with just two Fokker D IIIs and a solitary Albatros D I. Not surprisingly, Boelcke was not only the first to score, but had achieved seven victories before anyone else had claimed a solitary kill.

Boelcke was already highly decorated, being a recipient of the *Pour le Mérite*. He had 19 victories as a Fokker *Eindecker* pilot, and whilst guiding his fledglings in the new art of aerial warfare, Boelcke had taken his score to 40 confirmed kills by 28 October 1916 – the date he met his death. By then *Jasta* 2 had achieved more than 50 victories, with von Richthofen, Böhme and Leopold Reimann all becoming aces. The unit was now fully equipped with Albatros D IIs, and with the skies over the front always full of British aeroplanes, targets and victories were not difficult to come by.

Reading Boelcke's reports on his many combats, it seems as if both his, and his *Staffel's*, kills were as easily achieved as if they had been shooting at targets in a fair ground gallery. However, on 14 September 1916 he noted;

'Number 23 was a hard one. I had headed off the squadron he was with and picked the second one. He started to get away. The third attacked Ltn Reimann, and was soon engaged by Ltns Böhme and Reimann, but nevertheless escaped within his own lines. My opponent pretended to fall

Boelcke is seen about to fly his Albatros D II D.386/16. It carried no special markings, but did have leader's streamers trailing from the wings. Boelcke died in this machine (*HAC/UTD*)

after the first shots. I knew this trick and followed him closely. He was trying to reach his own lines but did not succeed. His wings broke off and the machine broke to pieces. As he fell so far behind our front I did not get a chance to inspect the wreck.

'After a short while I saw several Englishmen circling over P_____. When I got nearer they wanted to attack me. As I was lower, I paid no attention to them, but turned away. As they saw I would not fight, one of them attacked another German machine. I could not allow this to go so attacked him and he soon suffered for it. I shot up his fuel and oil tanks and wounded him in the thigh. He was forced to land and was captured. That was number 24.'

These kills took the form of a Sopwith 1½ Strutter two-seater and a DH 2 of Nos 70 and 24 Sqns respectively. Just over a month later Boelcke's score had reached 40.

Stephan Kirmaier took over command of *Jasta* 2 after Boelcke and flew this Albatros D II, its fuselage stained a reddish brown. While some pilots of this unit carried initials on their machines (including 'Hö' for Höhne and 'Bü' for Büttner), Kirmaier's D II simply wore a black vertical fuselage band forward of the cross and a black and white streamer fixed between the wing interplane struts (*HAC/UTD*)

On the fateful day that Germany's first great ace met his death, *Jasta* 2 found itself embroiled in yet another fight with the nimble DH 2s of No 24 Sqn. During the course of the whirling action, Böhme (who claimed 22 of his 24 victories with the *Jasta*) and Boelcke collided, and the 'master' fell to his death. His score of 40 victories weeks before the end of 1916 – 21 of them leading *Jasta* 2 – gives great credit to the man. Although the war was to continue for two more years, only a further nine German pilots were to exceed this tally, while two others equalled it.

One of these individuals was, of course, Manfred von Richthofen. We shall read of his exploits in a further volume in this series, dealing with the Fokker Dr 1 Triplane (a machine with which he is synonymous), but he achieved the bulk of his victories flying Albatros fighters. For all of 1917 he was the top scoring pilot in service, and although he claimed a few victories in the Halberstadt, the bulk were achieved in an Albatros.

He became known as the 'Red Baron', or 'Red Devil', because he painted his fighter red – or at least partially red. It has often been suggested that the 'red' was more maroon, with proponents of this theory stating that the surviving 'bits' of fabric from his final Dr I that are today held in museums prove their point. However, this difference in coloration has come about simply through the ageing process.

Once commanding *Jasta* 11, which he joined after his time with *Jasta* 2 (where he claimed 16 victories), von Richthofen had most of his *staffel's* machines adorned with red paint, whilst he personally flew either an all-red, or partial red, machine during important ground battles. He chose this colour so that his aircraft was quickly visible to his men should they need to locate him once in the air, and to enable ground observers to help confirm his claims.

Despite various suggestions to the contrary, von Richthofen's aircraft were indeed *red*, for there was no tactical benefit to be derived from using a darker colour. Having personally seen the actual red fabric of his last

Four of *Jasta* 2's pilots. They are, from left to right, Stephan Kirmaier, who took over from Boelcke after his death, Hans Imelmann (six victories, and killed in action on 3 January 1917), Manfred von Richthofen and Hans Wortmann (two victories, and killed in action on 2 April 1917). Behind them is an Albatros D II with a white nose band, which was apparently von Richthofen's – possibly D.481/16. Note the protective covers over the propeller blades. Wortmann is another pilot who appears to wear eye glasses. The field glasses round the Baron's neck were used by the great ace to keep a check on hostile aircraft over the front prior to take-off
(*G VanWyngarden collection*)

Future Fokker D VII ace Hermann Frommherz (left) stands with his mechanics in front of his *Blaue Maus* – the all-blue Albatros D III he used with *Jasta* 2 (Boelcke) (*P Grosz via G VanWyngarden*)

Line up of *Jasta* Boelcke's Albatros fighters. From left is Gerhard Bassenge's D III, next is an early D V with headrest, while third is Friedrich Kempf's D III, followed by Frommherz's pale blue D III. Note the white tails, which was *Jasta* 2's unit marking at this time (*G VanWyngarden collection*)

Fokker Triplane, there is no doubt in my mind that it resembled pillar-box red! It must be remembered that frontline *Jastas* did not have a massive selection of paints to choose from. Most paint – or dope – readily to hand was either green, mauve or brown in colour, as these were the three shades that made up the standard fighter camouflage throughout the war. Black and white, for national markings, was also in good supply, whilst other colours had to be obtained almost certainly through unofficial means. Pots of red and blue paint were sometimes 'liberated' from captured airfields used by British or French units, whilst other shades were obtained from Germany. Finally, standard colours were occasionally mixed to make a variety of different shades.

Although forever associated with von Richthofen, several other all-red aircraft could be found on the Western Front sometime before the ace's Albatros shot to fame – not the least of these being Jean Navarre's all-red Nieuport 11. There are many other cases of red aircraft being spotted over the battle zones in 1916-17, and into 1918. Of course, it did not harm von Richthofen's reputation that 'all' red aircraft were flown by him!

Jasta 2 produced 20 aces, with several more serving with the unit for a period during which they added to their overall score. The unit also 'fed' several other *Jastas* with seasoned and experienced leaders, taking the doctrines of Oswald Boelcke with them.

After Boelcke's death, Oblt Stefan Kirmaier took over command. The latter had three victories from his time flying *Eindeckers*, and his score had risen to 11 by the time he was killed fighting with DH 2s from No 24 Sqn on 22 November. Another early *Jasta* 2 ace of this period was Hans Imelmann, who had also seen combat with the Fokker, but had scored all six of his victories flying the Albatros with the former unit. He was killed in action with No 4 Sqn on 23 January 1917.

Max Müller (the von came later, following his death) also 'made ace' with *Jasta* 2, before taking his five victories with him to *Jasta* 28. Having

then brought his score to 29, winning the *Blue Max* in the process, he returned to *Jasta* 2 in November 1917, taking temporary command on 6 January 1918. Adding seven more kills to his tally, he then fell to observer fire from a Royal Aircraft Factory RE 8 three days later.

Otto Walter Höhne gained all six of his victories with *Jasta* 2 in 1916 following service as a Fokker pilot, and then a few days with *Jasta* 1. In January 1917 he was badly wounded in a fight with Sopwith 1¹/₂ Strutters that subsequently kept him away from the front for most of the year. Höhne finally returned to command *Jasta* 59 in December, and he even spent a few weeks in charge of *Jasta* 2 in January 1918, but he was never deemed fit enough to return to frontline flying again. He did, however, see action in World War 2, winning the Knight's Cross in the process, but he was again severely injured in a crash in August 1941 which put an end to his flying. Höhne finally died in 1969, aged 74.

Fritz Otto Bernert commanded *Jasta* 2 between June and August 1917, following service with *Jasta* 4. He joined the former unit having gained one victory as an *Eindecker* pilot and six more with *Jasta* 4, these victories being scored despite the fact that he enjoyed the use of only one good arm. Prior service in the trenches with the army had left him with a useless left arm following a bayonet wound, yet he had gone on to become a pilot and seen duty flying two-seaters, before finally joining the *Jastas*. What is more, he wore eye glasses!

During April 1917 – dubbed 'Bloody April' by the RFC – Bernert shot down 15 British aeroplanes, including a record five in one day on the 24th. Taking command of *Jasta* 6 in May, he increased his score to 27, then returned to command *Jasta* 2 but was wounded in combat on 18 August without having adding to his tally. The survivor of many sorties over the front, Bernert was fated to die in the great influenza epidemic of 1918, passing away on 18 October.

Gerhard Bassenge scored six victories. He is seen here sat upon his Albatros, which featured perpendicular black and white bands on a clear-varnished fuselage. The tail was white aft of the thin black band, and its upper wings a mix of light and dark green, with a reddish brown
(*via G VanWyngarden*)

Paul Bäumer enjoyed his first successes with *Jasta* 5 (three victories) in July 1917, before moving to *Jasta* 2. He remained with this unit until war's end, by which time he had scored an impressive 43 victories. Bäumer flew at least three Albatros Scouts – 4409/17, 4430/17 and 5410/17– during the summer and autumn of 1917, using them to increase his score to 18. One of the last recipients of the *Pour le Mérite* (his award was made just nine days before the Armistice), Bäumer was known as 'The Iron Eagle'. One of the first German fighter pilots to have his life saved by the employment of a parachute, in September 1918, he was eventually killed testing an aeroplane during an airshow in July 1927.

Paul Bäumer, flew with *Jasta* 5 between June and August 1917, then with *Jasta* 2 till the war's end. Awarded the *Pour le Mérite*, he achieved 43 victories

The other great Albatros ace within *Jasta* 2 was Werner Voss, whom we shall also meet in greater detail within the Fokker Dr I book in this series. Like von Richthofen, he too is better known for the (comparatively short) time he spent flying the Triplane, although the bulk of his kills came whilst he was serving with the Albatros scout-equipped *Jasta* 2, followed by *Jasta* 5. This former Hussar first saw service on the Eastern Front while still a teenager. He transferred to aviation in 1916 and flew two-seaters until arriving at *Jasta* 2 in November 1917. By early April 1917 Voss had scored a total of 22 victories, for which he received the *Pour le Mérite*. It was customary for a winner of the *Blue Max* to have a period of home leave, and Voss began his on 7 April, just as the Arras Offensive began. The weeks that followed produced the worst casualty figures suffered by the RFC in World War 1, and one can only imagine just how many more victories Voss may have scored had he remained at the front.

As it happened he did not return to the fighting until 5 May, yet during the rest of that month he added four more kills to his score before assuming command of *Jasta* 5. This unit was yet another of the great Ger-

Werner Voss used this distinctively marked Albatros D III whilst with *Jasta* 2 in 1917. For full colour details of this aircraft see profile five, and the associated plate commentary in the appendices. Voss's aircraft is also depicted on the cover of this volume

man fighting *Jastas* of World War 1, and Voss had scored six more victories whilst serving as its *Staffelführer* when he was grabbed by von Richthofen to command *Jasta* 10, which was part of the Baron's JG I (*Jastas* 4, 6, 10 and 11). Voss's arrival at *Jasta* 10 came at almost the same moment as the first Fokker Triplanes appeared at the front, and his short career with this aircraft will be detailed in the *Aircraft of the Aces* volume on the Dr I.

JASTA 3

Jasta 3 produced just six aces of its own, the first of these being Ltn Alfred Mohr. Sadly, nothing is known of his background, but he must have been experienced for he was given command of the newly-formed *Jasta* soon after its first CO was killed, although at that point Mohr was still to score his first success. He was eventually killed on 1 April 1917 during combat with a Royal Aircraft Factory BE 2 from No 12 Sqn, his Albatros D III (2012/16) coming down behind British lines. Mohr had scored six kills by the time of his death.

Another early ace was Ltn Georg Schlenker, who was already serving in the army when war broke out. Volunteering for aviation, he initially spent time as a two-seater pilot, prior to joining *Jasta* 3 at the beginning of September 1916. He did not gain his first success until the following January, but by April he had scored seven victories. Schlenker joined *Jasta* 41 as its leader in late 1917, and had achieved 14 victories by the time a severe wound put him out of the war the following year.

Ltn Julius Schmidt had the unusual distinction of claiming his first victory whilst flying with KG 4, prior to joining *Jasta* 3 at the start of April 1917. By 14 September he had scored 15 confirmed kills, and although he claimed his 16th on this day, it remained unconfirmed due to the

British pilot successfully carrying out a forced landing in Allied-held territory. Schmidt's opponent on this day was almost certainly Lt A P F Rhys Davids DSO, MC of No 56 Sqn, who was to shoot down Werner Voss just nine days later. Twenty-four hours after Voss's death, Schmidt himself was so badly wounded in an engagement with Camels of No 70 Sqn that he did not see any further action.

Also involved in the Rhys Davids fight with Schmidt was fellow Albatros ace Carl Menckhoff, although he did have his SE 5 claim from this action upheld. Unlike many of his contemporaries, this Westphalian was no youngster, having turned 34 by the time he shot down his first (British) aeroplane. Menckhoff had briefly served as a soldier as long ago as 1903, and he had rejoined upon the outbreak of war in 1914. He was soon wounded in action, and upon recovering transferred to the air service, where he became a pilot on the Russian Front. After a period as an instructor, and in spite of his age, he was assigned to fighters and went to *Jasta* 3 in early 1917. By the end of the year Menckhoff's score had risen to 18 victories, and he added two more in 1918 flying the Albatros – by which time he had been posted to *Jasta* 72 as its commander. By war's end he had achieved 39 kills, many of the latter whilst at the controls of a Fokker D VII.

Ltn Kurt Wissemann's rise to fame came a few days after claiming a SPAD on 11 September 1917, which gave him his fifth victory. His opponent on this day was the great French ace, Georges Guynemer, who failed to return to base. A former soldier and air observer, Wissemann had been wounded while on two-seaters, but had nonetheless gone on to become a pilot, being assigned to *Jasta* 3 at the end of May 1917. He did not get to bathe in his success over Guynemer for long, however, for he was himself killed when his scout was shot down by No 56 Sqn on 28 September.

Carl Menckhoff on his *Jasta 3* Albatros D V. It is camouflaged in cloudy hues of probably brown, olive green and mauve. A black or possibly red 'M' served as his personal marking. As far as is known, the *Jasta* had no unit marking at this period. By the end of 1917 Menckhoff had scored 18 victories. Awarded the *Pour le Mérite*, he later commanded *Jasta 72* and increased his tally to 39 before he was brought down and taken prisoner on 25 July 1918 (*G VanWyngarden collection*)

JASTA 4

A part of von Richthofen's JG I from June 1917, *Jasta* 4 was a high-scoring unit with nearly 200 kills. Aside from Otto Bernert, whom we have already covered, another of the *Jasta's* early aces was Ltn Wilhelm Frankl. A native of Hamburg who had learnt to fly pre-war, he still began his war as an observer in an *abteilung* unit, where he gained a victory with carbine fire in May 1915! In the early months of the following year Frankl began flying *Eindeckers*, and he scored a further eight kills (and won the *Pour le Mérite*) prior to joining *Jasta* 4. On 7 April 1917 he shot down his 20th opponent, this tally including the unique claim of a night kill over a Royal Aircraft Factory FE 2b from No 100 Sqn on 6 April. Two days later he was killed in a fight with Bristol Fighters when his Albatros D III (2158/16) fell to pieces in the air.

Kurt Wüsthoff flew this black spiral-marked Albatros D III (OAW) with *Jasta* 4 in 1917. It features dark grey or even black wheel covers, and otherwise standard camouflage. The black spiral band around the fuselage was the unit marking of *Jasta* 4 (*G VanWyngarden collection*)

Another *Jasta 4 Pour le Mérite* winner was Hans Klein. This former soldier had also been an *Eindecker* pilot, although he had failed to score any confirmed victories until he joined *Jasta* 4 in April 1917. His third kill, on 8 April, was, like Frankl's on the 6th, a night victory – yet another No 100 Sqn FE 2. Wounded on 13 July 1917 (probably by a pilot from No 29 Sqn, flying a Nieuport), upon recovery Klein took command of another JG I unit, *Jasta* 10, following the loss of Werner Voss. He had increased his score to 22 by November, but then had his right thumb shot away in combat on 19 February 1918 and saw no further operational flying.

Rittmeister Kurt von Döring had been a dragoon pre-war, but he had also learnt to fly prior to the outbreak of hostilities. Piloting two-seaters in the first years of the war, he eventually ended up with *Jasta* 4 in April 1917 as its *Staffelführer*. Von Döring retained this position until January 1918, and during this time he also occasionally relieved von Richthofen of the command of JG I while the latter was on leave from the front. He gained at least five victories flying the Albatros Scout, but by late 1918 his unit had converted to Fokker Triplanes. With a score of nine, von Döring took command of *Jagdgruppe* Nr. 4 and, later in 1918, commanded *Jasta* 66 and then *Jasta* 1. He ended the war with 11 victories.

From Aachen, Ltn Kurt Wüsthoff gained his pilot's certificate when he was just 16, and being too young for frontline service, became an instructor instead. Once old enough, he flew two-seaters in Bulgaria, Rumania, Macedonia and Greece, before returning to France in 1917 and joining *Jasta* 4. He gained several of his eventual 27 victories on the Albatros Scout during this time, and for a while he commanded the *Jasta*, prior to being assigned to the staff of JG I in March 1918. Wüsthoff did not see further combat except for being shot down in someone else's Fokker D VII and being taken prisoner on 17 June – the day after he had taken command of *Jasta* 15.

Silesian Oskar Freiherr von Boenigk had become an army cadet at the tender age of 11, and was subsequently commissioned in 1912 when he turned 18. Twice wounded in the trenches, he transferred to aviation and flew as an observer prior to becoming a pilot. By the early summer of 1917 von Boenigk was a part of *Jasta* 4, with whom he gained at least five victories on Albatros Scouts. He then went to *Jasta* 21 as *Staffelführer*, before later commanding JG II. Of von Boenigk's 26 victories, most were claimed on Fokker D VIIs, but at least five were scored flying Albatros Scouts.

JASTA 5

Another big-scoring unit, *Jasta* 5 claimed over 250 victories. It had some exceptional pilots on its strength, none more so than its first commander,

Edmund Nathanael of *Jasta* 5 scored 15 victories in 1917 before his death in combat on 11 May. He was shot down by Capt C K Cochrane-Patrick MC of No 23 Sqn, who was flying a SPAD

Jasta 5's Otto Könnecke (second from left) poses with his ground-crewmen in front of his Albatros D V at Boistrancourt aerodrome in the summer of 1917. At this stage the personal black and white chequer-board with red border has been painted on the mostly green fuselage, but the spinner has not yet been painted red, nor has the red border been applied to the green tail. The underside of the fuselage remained unpainted varnished ply-wood (*G VanWyngarden collection*)

Hans Berr. A pre-war soldier who, like so many others, joined the air service after being wounded in the trenches, Berr first saw action as an observer. He then graduated to flying an *Eindecker*, scoring two victories with the Avillers Fokker *Staffel*. When this unit became the nucleus of *Jasta* 5 he was made its first commander, and by early November he had raised his score to ten and won the *Pour le Mérite*. Berr's promising career was cut short on 6 April 1917 – Good Friday – when his Albatros struck a second *Jasta* 5 machine during an attack on an FE 2b. Both men fell to their deaths. Werner Voss, as already recorded, then assumed command of the unit.

Ltn Hans Karl Müller was another early ace within *Jasta* 5. A Saxon who had already scored single victories with a two-seater unit and a Fokker *Staffel*, he had taken his score to nine with *Jasta* 5 by Christmas 1916. However, he was severely wounded on 26 December, and did not see any further frontline service. Müller survived the war as a test pilot, and he later emigrated to Mexico, where he ran a flying school.

Ltn Renatus Theiller was another pre-war pilot who then saw war service with two-seater units prior to joining *Jasta* 5. His first two victories were claimed whilst flying with the *abteilung* units, and he rapidly increased his tally once he was given an Albatros Scout to fly by his new *Jasta*. Having taken his tally to 12, Theiller was killed on 24 March 1917, his Albatros D III was shot down in combat with No 70 Sqn's Sopwith 1¹/2 Strutters.

Heinrich Gontermann would become one of the highest scoring German scout pilots, and he started his career with *Jasta* 5. A former Uhlan cavalryman, he was wounded early in the war and moved into aviation upon recovery. After a period as both a pilot and observer on two-seaters, he transferred to fighters in November 1916. He joined *Jasta* 5, and within days Gontermann had claimed his first kill, and he continued to steadily increase his score during the spring of 1917. By the end of 'Bloody April' his tally had reached 17.

Promoted to command *Jasta* 15, Gontermann had taken his tally to 39 victories by early October, although by this time he was flying one of the new Fokker Triplanes. However, most of his claims were scored at the

Line up of *Jasta* 5's flamboyantly decorated Albatros D Vs, and a few D IIIs, at Boistrancourt aerodrome in the summer of 1917. Third from right is the red dragon machine first flown by Oblt Richard Flasher (CO) and later by Hans von Hippel, who survived the loss of a lower wing in this aircraft on 18 February 1918. Fourth from right is Rumey's 'demon head', while fourth from the end is Könnecke's D V
(*G VanWyngarden collection*)

This Albatros D V was flown by Fritz Rumey in *Jasta* 5. While not a brilliant photo, is does show the black and white candy stripes to good effect. Note too that even the struts and wheel covers were painted alternatively black and white – all designed to throw off the aim of a pursuing pilot by optical illusion. The two white stripes on the green horizontal tailplane were unique to Rumey's machine (*G VanWyngarden collection*)

This Albatros D V is marked with a ferocious 'demon-head', and was probably flown by Fritz Rumey at one time. Close inspection shows the fuselage is painted in a faint two-colour chequerboard pattern, although the colours are not known. Rumey stands second from the left, while Josef Mai is on the far right (*G VanWyngarden collection*)

controls of an Albatros Scout, and these included the destruction of 17 kite balloons. On 19 August 1917 Gontermann shot down a SPAD in the morning and then four balloons in four minutes that evening, which beat his previous record of two balloons on three or four earlier occasions. Having forsaken his Albatros for a Triplane, Gontermann had seen little action with the Fokker fighter. He was killed on 30 October in a crash caused by the separation of the top wing of his Triplane – a number of early Dr Is were lost in similar circumstances.

Edmund Nathanael had received decorations for bravery before becoming a fighter pilot, gaining the General Honour Decoration in Gold with Swords, and the rarely issued Wilhelm Ernst War Cross from the Duchy of Saxe-Weimer, while flying two-seaters. Once with *Jasta* 5 he claimed 15 victories in exactly two months (March to May 1917), including the first SE 5 to be lost by the RFC, on 30 April. In turn, Nathanael was shot down and killed 11 days later by RFC SPAD ace, Capt C K Cochrane-Patrick, of No 23 Sqn.

Kurt Schneider almost duplicated Nathanael's fighting career, winning the Iron Cross 2nd Class with the army, prior to becoming a pilot with *Jasta* 5 in August 1916. However, he did not score his first kill until March 1917, but had run up a tally of 15 by 28 May. Wounded in combat with FE 2s of No 22 Sqn on 5 June, Schneider returned in July, only to be shot down again in Albatros D V 1066/17, but this time he succumbed to his injuries. By the time of his death Schneider had received the Iron Cross 1st Class and the Albert Order Knight 2nd Class with Swords. He was awarded a posthumous Knight's Cross of the Military St Henry Order.

Although legendary ace Werner Voss joined *Jasta* 5 in the early summer of 1917, it was three NCO pilots who made names for themselves during this period – Otto Könnecke, Fritz Rumey and Josef Mai. Könnecke, a pre-war soldier, learnt to fly in 1913 and initially served as an instructor, before going to Macedonia to fly with *Jasta* 25. Gaining three victories in early 1917, he was sent back to France to join *Jasta* 5, and by the end of the year his score had risen to 11. Könnecke survived the war with a tally of 35 kills, having been awarded the *Pour le Mérite* two months prior to the Armistice.

Fritz Rumey was another former pre-war soldier, and he first saw action on the Russian Front. After a period as a two-seat observer, he

Two 'old bones' ('old hands') of *Jasta* 5 – veterans Rumey and Mai – received these two D Vas that had been experimentally fitted with Siemens 'motor' machine-guns capable of a cyclic rate of fire of 1400 rounds a minute. They were not allowed to fly over the lines in them, but it is known that some German pilots achieved victories with such guns. Mai's machine is on the left and Rumey's on the right. The civilian is Herr Kaendler, an engineer from the Siemens Works (*Dresden Armee Museum/Grosz/via G VanWyngarden collection*)

Josef Mai with his *Jasta* 5 Albatros D Va, marked with the star and crescent. It features a red spinner and nose band and some unusual mottling on the top fuselage decking – probably light brown and dark green. Its wings are covered in lozenge fabric, with light rib tapes in either blue or salmon pink. Mai's three mechanics are Klöckner, Zahn and Schumacher (*G VanWyngarden collection*)

became a pilot and was posted to France. Following a brief stay with *Jasta* 2, Rumey went to *Jasta* 5, with whom he scored his first kill on 6 July 1917. He would eventually be credited with 45 victories, the first few of which were claimed flying Albatros Scouts before he moved on to the Triplane and, finally, the Fokker D VII in 1918. Also a *Blue Max* winner, Rumey was killed on 27 September 1918 when his parachute failed to open after he had baled out of his Fokker fighter following a collision with a British aeroplane.

The last of the trio, Josef Mai became a pilot in 1916, and following service with *Kasta* 29, he moved to *Jasta* 5 as a fighter pilot in March 1917. Like Könnecke, he too scored 11 victories with Albatros Scouts (four in D V 2082/17 and seven in D Va 5284/17) before the unit re-equipped with Triplanes and eventually D VIIs. Mai remained with the *Jasta* till war's end, by which time he had won the *Pour le Mérite* and seen his tally reach 30 victories. He finally passed away in 1982 at the age of 94.

A former Saxon field artillery officer who saw action in France and Russia, Ltn Rudolf Matthaei then transferred to the infantry on the Western Front, prior to joining the air service in 1916. After the usual period on two-seaters, he arrived at *Jasta* 21 in February 1917, where he scored three confirmed victories. Moving to *Jasta* 5 in the spring, he became an ace on 20 August. By the end of the year Matthaei had been credited with nine kills, and he added one more whilst serving as commander of *Jasta* 46 in February 1918. However, this was to be his last success, for he was killed in a flying accident in April.

JASTA 6

Jasta 6 produced a dozen aces, the first of these being Vfw Fritz Krebs, who joined the unit in May 1917. In a brief career, he shot down eight British aeroplanes before falling to the guns of Capt G H Bowman of No 56 Sqn.

By this date Otto Bernert had come and gone (as detailed earlier in this chapter), and the new CO, Eduard von Dostler, had arrived from *Jasta* 34, where he had scored

Albatros D V D.1060/17 of *Jasta* 6 may have been the aircraft flown by Oblt Eduard Dostler. It has two black (or blue?) bands aft of the cockpit and a black nose and wheels. Note, however, that it lacks the black and white tail stripes of *Jasta* 6 (*G VanWyngarden collection*)

Hans Adam, leader of *Jasta* 6, scored 21 victories before falling in combat on 15 November 1917 in Albatros D V D.5222/17. He was shot down in a fight with Nos 29 and 45 Sqns, the destruction of his aircraft being credited to Lt K B Montgomery from the latter unit

On 2 August 1917 Hans Adam crashed this Albatros D V (D.1148/17) on landing, although he survived unhurt. The black and white tail stripes of *Jasta* 6 are clearly in evidence, and Adam's personal marking of a black fuselage band, edged white, is also visible. Note too the underwing stripes (*G VanWyngarden collection*)

Jasta 7 pilots in November 1917. Seated in the central position is unit leader, Josef Jacobs, who was well known for flying black-painted aircraft. Hermann Kunz is to his right. Standing second from the right is Paul Billik, who would score a total of 31 victories, most as leader of *Jasta* 52. Fourth from right is Paul Lotz, who claimed nine victories, four with *Jasta* 7 and five as leader of *Jasta* 44. Seventh from right is Oberflugmeister Kurt Schonfelder, who was a naval pilot serving with the unit. He scored 13 victories. Finally, eighth from right is Carl Degelow, who claimed two victories with *Jasta* 7 and 28 more as leader of *Jasta* 40

This *Jasta* 22 line up was photographed in early 1917. Second from the right is the LVG-built Albatros D II (D.1072/16) flown by Josef Jacobs, and marked with his nickname, *KOBES*. The other machines also carry personal markings, and note the reflection of the nearest aircraft's fuselage stripes on the underside of the upper wing (*HAC/UTD via G VanWyngarden collection*)

eight kills. A Bavarian, with pre-war soldiering service behind him, he had been inspired to leave the trenches and take up flying when his pilot brother had been killed in action. Von Dostler gained his first victory as a two-seater pilot in late 1916, before moving onto fighters, firstly with *Jasta* 13 and then 34b. He assumed command of *Jasta* 6 on 10 June 1917, and scored heavily over the next eight weeks, winning the *Pour le Mérite* and taking his total to 26 by 18 August. Three days later von Dostler intercepted an RE 8 over the front but was shot down and killed by its defensive fire. He subsequently received a posthumous Bavarian Military Max-Joseph Order, which gave him the rank of knight (Ritter).

The now vacant position of commander of *Jasta* 6 was duly filled by another already successful Albatros pilot, Hans Adam, who had also served with *Jasta* 34b (where he scored three victories flying Albatros D III 2102/16), and who had been flying under Dostler since mid-July 1917. When the latter fell on 21 August 1917, Adam had scored 12 victories, and by early November his tally had risen to 21. Another Bavarian, he was over 30 years old, married and with two children.

Following a familiar career path for a German fighter pilot, Adam had been wounded in the infantry in 1914, then became an observer and finally a pilot. He also became Ritter von Adam with the award of the Military Max-Joseph Order, but was killed in action on 15 November 1917 when shot down by Lt K B Montgomery, flying a No 45 Sqn Camel.

The next *Staffelführer* at *Jasta* 6 was Wilhelm Reinhard, posted in from *Jasta* 11 – by this time, of course, the former unit was part of JG I. From Dusseldorf, Willi Reinhard had been a pre-war soldier and had also been wounded in the early months of the conflict. Joining the air service, he served his time on two-seaters prior to undertaking fighter training, and joined *Jasta* 11 in June 1917. By the time he moved to command *Jasta* 6, Reinhard had claimed six victories, although it is not possible to ascertain how many other victories he claimed on Albatros Scouts, for many of his

Hermann Kunz of *Jasta* 7 flew this black Albatros Scout marked with a white swastika marking in 1917. He scored three victories and later became an ace with *Jasta* 1(F) in Palestine in 1918

subsequent kills were achieved flying Triplanes. In April 1918 he was made commander of JG I following von Richthofen's death, and by mid-June his score had reached 20. Never bested in combat, Reinhard was killed testing a new fighter at Aldershof on 18 June.

JASTA 7

Only three Albatros aces of note were produced by *Jasta* 7, the most successful of whom was Josef Jacobs, who ended the war with an impressive 48 victories. Prior to joining the unit, he had flown *Eindeckers*, gaining his first victory with the Fokker fighter in 1916. With the coming of the *Jastas* he was assigned to *Jasta* 22, with whom he claimed another four kills confirmed, as well as several unconfirmed, before transferring to *Jasta* 7 as its commander in August 1917. Jacobs scored steadily during the remaining weeks of summer, and then into the early autumn, raising his total to a dozen by the end of the year. The arrival of the Fokker Triplane at the front in October resulted in Jacobs forsaking his Albatros Scout for the Dr I, and he continued to fly the latter fighter long after it had been withdrawn from most frontline units.

The only other high scorer within *Jasta* 7 was Vfw Friedrich Manschott, who gained his first victory on two-seaters in 1916. He joined the *Jasta* in January 1917, and in less than three months had scored a total of 12 victories, including three balloons. Manschott was killed in action on 16 March during a fight with four French machines.

Naval pilot Obfg Kurt Schönfelder is also believed to have become an ace flying Albatros Scouts with *Jasta* 7. Having learnt to fly in 1913, he joined the unit in early 1917 and was credited with his first confirmed kill on 20 July 1917 – his previous three claims had all remained unconfirmed. In 1918 Schönfelder transitioned to the Fokker D VII (by which time he had undoubtedly become an ace on the Albatros), and he was eventually shot down and killed by Lt Ken Unger, and others, from No 210 Sqn on 26 June.

JASTA 8

Oblt zur See Konrad Mettlich commanded *Jasta* 8 from 29 July 1917 until his death in combat with No 84 Sqn SE 5as on 13 March 1918 – during this time he gained six victories. As can be seen from his rank, he was also a naval officer, and had been an *Eindecker* pilot in 1916. He then transferred into *Marine Jagdstaffel* Nr. 1 in 1917, before being sent to *Jasta* 8 in June, prior to taking command.

Jasta 8's first ace was Walter Göttsch. From Hamburg, he too had flown two-seaters prior to becoming a fighter pilot, arriving at *Jasta* 8 on 10 September 1916. His first kill was a Belgian kite balloon, and his fifth and sixth claims came on 1 February 1917. Two days later he was wounded in a fight with FE 2b 'pushers' of No 20 Sqn, the latter unit having waged a personal war with *Jasta* 8 during the opening weeks of the new year. Indeed Götsch's first FE victory back on 7 January had been over a No 20 Sqn aircraft, and had resulted in its pilot, Flt Sgt Tom Mottershead DCM, winning a posthumous Victoria Cross.

Götsch's combat on the afternoon of 1 February can be viewed via the combat report lodged by Lts J K Stead and W T Jourdan from No 20 Sqn. In part, the latter officer recorded;

'I sighted one H.A. (hostile aircraft) climbing to the rear of (the) formation, well under and to the side of the right-hand machine. I notified my pilot and kept an eye on H.A., who did not seem to be in a hurry to attack. About this time I noticed a second H.A. doing the same manoeuvre on our left side, and as the first two H.A. met well to our rear and high above, a third H.A. joined them about the same position; it was then that I noticed a fourth H.A. well below us, who dived towards Courtrai, at the same time, one of the three H.A. fired a red light. H.A. changed his course and dived on our right rear machine. At this time all three H.A. were out of my range so I stood by my gun to await the next move.

Jasta 9's Hartmut Baldamus was photographed in his Albatros in early 1917. One of the early Albatros aces, he achieved a total of 18 victories before colliding with a French fighter and falling to his death on 14 April 1917. Note pistol flares in their holder forward of the cockpit

'. . . the H.A. that dived on our right rear machine manoeuvred in front of our machine, discharging a burst of bullets, one of which wounded my pilot in the right leg. I then engaged this H.A. with the gun on (the) rear mounting. I believe my bullets registered on his machine. The two machines in the rear still held their place and did not molest us as he held our height and course. My pilot, bleeding furiously, and we being so far from the lines, had no alternative but to fire a green light and to abandon the combat. On the way to the lines, the pilot saw one of our machines descending in flames but looked under control.

'I kept my pilot from collapsing from loss of blood by strapping up his right leg as tight as possible with a short strap I had with me.'

The FE recovered at No 1 Sqn's base, where the pilot fainted soon after landing, having had an artery severed in his right leg. Lt Jourdan also discovered that their auxiliary fuel tank had been holed. No 20 Sqn lost two FEs to Walter Göttsch that afternoon. He had taken his tally to 12 before he was wounded once again during yet another engagement with this unit on 29 June, although he was back in action by mid-July. Two months later, with his score at 17, Göttsch was wounded by No 20 Sqn for a third time, although by now the RFC unit was flying the considerably more capable Bristol F 2b Fighter.

Moving to *Jasta* 19 as leader in 1918, Göttsch had increased his score to 20 flying a Triplane by the time he was killed in action on 10 April, hit by return fire from his final claim.

Rudolf Franke had been a *Schutzstaffel* pilot before going initially to *Jasta* 2 in early 1917, and then moving on to *Jasta* 8 just weeks later. His first eight victories were scored in 1917, and he continued to add to his tally (which eventually reached 15) in 1918, although by this time he was flying Fokker D VIIs.

Wilhelm Seitz claimed his first kill with the *Jasta* in 1916, but had to wait until March 1918 to score his all important fifth kill. By the time he left to command *Jasta* 68 in September, his total stood at 11, to which he had added five more by war's end.

Aloys Heldmann joined *Jasta* 10 in November 1916, and was still with the unit at war's end. In early 1917 he flew a yellow-nosed Albatros D V with a light blue tail and black fuselage band. In all Heldmann achieved 15 victories, several of which were scored with the Albatros. He is seen here posing alongside a Pfalz D III

Jasta 10 lined up at Marcke in 1917. Individual markings are various, including Erich Löwenhardt's D III (OAW) with a white snake line on fuselage and upper wing, Adam Barth's white dumb-bell marking, Paul Aue's white circle round the cockpit area and Vfw Burggaller's D III with a white bar. Aloys Heldmann's machine is on the far left (*G VanWyngarden collection*)

Rudolf Wendelmuth transferred to aviation from the infantry in 1915, and he first saw action on the Bulgarian and Turkish Fronts, where he achieved one combat victory in November 1916. Posted to *Jasta* 8 in France, he scored ten more kills before being given command of *Jasta* 20 in October. Having increased his score to 14, Wendelmuth lost his life on 30 November when his fighter collided with a machine from *Jasta* 4. The pilot from the latter unit was also killed.

JASTA 9

Twenty-four-year-old Hartmut Baldamus, from Dresden, was an ace before he even arrived at *Jasta* 9, having seen extensive action with a two-seater unit which almost certainly employed a small flight of fighters for protection. He was then sent to *Jasta* 9 in November 1916, and by the beginning of January he had become a double-ace. During the early months of 1917 Baldamus increased his score to 18, and although he participated in 'Bloody April', most of his patrols were flown along the French Front. His final victory was scored by collision, the claim being lodged by his fellow pilots, for Baldamus did not survive the impact between his Albatros and a French Nieuport Scout.

Another *Jasta* 9 ace was Heinrich Kroll, whose first five claims were all against French SPADs during May 1917 – the last of these was flown by French ace Rene Dorme, who claimed 23 victories. The son of a Kiel schoolmaster, Kroll was himself training to teach when he decided instead to join the army as a fusilier. Transferring to aviation in January 1916, he completed the mandatory period on two-seaters prior to joining his first *Jasta*.

Following his successful spell with *Jasta* 9, Kroll took command of *Jasta* 24 in August 1917. He had endured many scraps during his time in the frontline, including being shot down in flames on 27 July, and by the end of 1917 his score stood at 15 victories. More kills followed in 1918, and by the summer Kroll's tally had reached 33, most of which had been claimed flying a succession of Albatros Scouts. He had received the *Pour le Mérite* in March, but was wounded on 14 August, and this injury put him out of the war.

Jasta 9's Ltn Fritz Pütter also gained 'acedom' on the Albatros, and despite eventually destroying 25 aircraft before being killed in a non-combat related flying accident in August 1918, he was a slow starter.

Von Althaus (right) with Otto Bernert, who gained 27 victories with *Jastas* 4, 2 and 6, before wounds took him away from operational flying, but not before he had won the *Blue Max*. Bernert flew with spectacles, a not unusual occurrence in amongst German pilots in World War 1

Having gained a field commission with the army on the Russian Front, he eventually chose to become a fighter pilot. A spell on two-seaters followed, before he joined *Jasta* 9 in March 1917. Pütter claimed his first victory on 14 April when he downed a balloon – indeed, his first five victories were all balloons, destroying two in August and a further pair on 1 November. By the time he left to command *Jasta* 68 in February 1918, Pütter's score had risen to ten, seven of which were balloons. Winner of the *Pour le Mérite,* most of his kills would have been scored flying the Albatros, for the Fokker D VII had only just started to arrive in the front-line when he was killed flying an early example.

JASTA 10

Jasta 10 was the third unit within von Richthofen's JG I, and it had achieved only a modest score (four or five kills in all) prior to June 1917. Two of its early pilots were Erich Löwenhardt and Alois Heldmann, both of whom would later become aces, and the former a *Blue Max* winner.

The son of a doctor, Löwenhardt came from Breslau, where he had been a cadet pre-war. He saw much action as an infantryman in the east during the first months of the conflict, being decorated for saving the lives of five soldiers. Commissioned soon afterwards, Löwenhardt was eventually wounded and sent back to Germany. Whilst recuperating, he decided to join the air service, and he arrived at *Jasta* 10 in March 1917, via two-seaters. Getting off to a slow start, and enjoying some lucky escapes in Albatros fighters in his first few months with the unit, Löwenhardt had nonetheless scored five kills by the time the first Dr Is arrived at *Jasta* 10. Most of his subsequent victories came flying the Fokker D VII, his score reaching 54 before a mid-air collision ended his life.

Like Löwenhardt, Aloys Heldmann served as an infantryman on the Eastern Front prior to learning to fly. He then spent time on the Serbian and Bulgarian Fronts, before finally arriving in France. Joining *Jasta* 10 in November 1916, Heldmann failed to achieve a confirmed victory until July 1917, and although he later scored a total of 15 kills (many on Pfalz D types and Fokkers), he is thought to have gained at least five in the Albatros.

ALBATROS D V AND D Va

By the early months of 1917 the Albatros D II had disappeared from frontline *Jastas*, leaving the D III to assume the position of dominant German fighter. Outwardly, the latter design looked very similar to the D II except for one major change which centred on the shape of the lower wing. At the request of senior officers within the air service, Albatros designers *Dipl-Ing* Robert Thelen and *Dipl-Ing* Schubert had adopted the sesquiplane wing layout used to such good effect by the French Nieuport Scout. As a consequence of the lower flying surface having been greatly reduced in chord, the D III's two wing struts had to be modified into a V-strut layout.

The new wing layout of the Albatros mirrored the French design to such a degree that British combat reports from this period often mention pilots encountering German 'Nieuport-type' fighters, and later they were also referred to as 'Vee-Strutters'. The main advantage of the narrower lower wing, of course, was the greatly improved downward visibility enjoyed by the pilot.

In May 1917 the first D Vs began arriving at the front, this aircraft being referred to as a 'lightened D III' by Albatros. Despite its reduced weight, the new fighter did not give the *Jasta* pilots much of a combat advantage over the vastly improving Allied fighters. Indeed, the high command realised that the D V could not hope for the technical superiority its predecessors from Albatros had enjoyed over its foes from mid-1916 through to the spring of 1917. Instead, they hoped that improved construction techniques associated with the new fighter would allow an increased number of aircraft to be supplied to the *Jastas*, who in turn would use these to numerically overwhelm the opposition.

The main recognition feature of the D V was its rounded fuselage and rudder, whilst 'under the skin' there were other improvements like aileron cables enclosed in the upper wing. Despite these modifications, the D V still had a propensity for breaking up when held in a prolonged dive, which created more than a little unease amongst its pilots.

The follow-on D Va was virtually identical to the D V except that the aileron controls reverted to the exposed system used with the D III. Therefore, in appearance the only visual difference between a D V and a D Va was the exposed aileron control wires on the former – something that an Allied pilot would care little about, and look for even less! Early D Vs were also seen with a large headrest, but as this tended to restrict the pilot's rearward vision, it was soon discarded.

With the arrival of the D V/Vas, a *Jasta* could now have three different types of Albatros fighter on strength at the same time. Since they could also be operating Pfalz D IIIs and, during the autumn of 1917 and again in early 1918, some Fokker Dr Is as well, it is often difficult to know for certain which types a pilot flew on a daily basis. New arrivals on a *Jasta* would usually be given the older machines, be they Albatros or Pfalz, to fly, and only if they survived combat (and any structural problems) and gained experience might they progress to a newer, and perhaps better performing, fighter.

JASTA 11

Jasta 11 has long been a part of fighter legend due both to its second commander, and because it was to become the highest scoring of all the *Jagdstaffeln* with 350 kills. Its first leader scored no victories. Indeed, from its formation date in October 1916 till the arrival of Manfred von Richthofen from *Jasta* 2 in January 1917, its score remained nil.

Von Richthofen arrived having recently been awarded the *Pour le Mérite*, and with 16 victories. He joined the *Jasta* on the 20th and made the first kill with his new unit just three days later – an FE 8 of No 40 Sqn, flown by Australian 2Lt John Hay, who was killed. There can be no doubt that von Richthofen had learnt a great deal from Oswald Boelcke, and what is more, he was able to instil into his new charges the hunting spirit that had dominated Boelcke's *Jasta* 2 pilots. As the winter weather improved towards spring, so von Richthofen honed his own skills, and those of his men. Leading from the front, March saw *Jasta* 11 down 28 British aeroplanes, whilst April began with a further 24 destroyed in the first eight days. The Rittmeister himself downed his 38th and 39th victories (a Sopwith 1¹/2 Strutter from No 43 Sqn and a BE 2g of No 16 Sqn) on the 8th.

A number of factors contributed to making 'Bloody April' such a one-sided contest in favour of the *Jastas*. Firstly, the *Jagdflieger* found no shortage of targets, for at this pivotal moment the skies were full of Allied

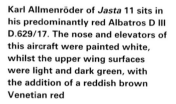

Karl Allmenröder of *Jasta* 11 sits in his predominantly red Albatros D III D.629/17. The nose and elevators of this aircraft were painted white, whilst the upper wing surfaces were light and dark green, with the addition of a reddish brown Venetian red

aeroplanes – particularly on the British Front – as the build up for the Battle of Arras had begun during March, and culminated in the Battle itself (the first big Allied offensive of 1917), which commenced on 9 April. Secondly, by April the newly-formed *Jastas* had become fully established on the Western Front, and with the winter weather having now passed, they were being given the first opportunity to employ new tactics for a sustained period of time. Finally, Allied fighters were fast becoming obsolete, and despite new designs having been promised to the RFC in France, it was going to be some months before SE 5s and Camels would make their presence felt. The French had their SPAD VIIs and, of course, they and the British were happy with their various Nieuports (see *Osprey Aircraft of the Aces 33 - Nieuport Scout Aces of World War 1*), but the RFC's DH 2s, FE 8s and Pups were no real match for the Albatros Scouts.

In the following few weeks the *Jagdflieger* had a field day, and *Jasta*

Lothar von Richthofen sits in the cockpit of his Albatros D III in 1917. His brother Manfred had 'handed this down' to him shortly after he arrived on *Jasta* 11, the 'Red Baron' having used it to score a number of his victories. The pilot on the ladder is believed to be Karl Allmenröder. The machine has a large red band around the fuselage just aft of the cockpit. Otherwise, it had the usual yellowish varnished fuselage and clear doped rudder *(G VanWyngarden collection)*

11 excelled even themselves. Manfred von Richthofen, now joined by his younger brother Lothar, together with such pilots as Karl Schäfer, Kurt Wolff, Karl Allmenröder and Sebastian Festner, cut a veritable swathe through the RFC flyers. The Baron knew the value of being able to identify aircraft in the air, and his all-red Albatros was an easy rallying point. His pilots also had areas of red on their machines, but with an individual colour to denote each man. Lothar used yellow, Wolff green, Schäfer black and Allmenröder white. Often, there was a reason for the markings worn on a pilot's aircraft, and more often than not it would refer to the colour of a former army regiment or cavalry squadron.

Aside from assisting recognition in the air, these colours helped front-line observers identify which German aeroplane had shot down which Allied machine. With the competition between pilots to gain victories and therefore honours and decorations, it was far easier for a non-aviator to confirm that a red and white aeroplane had indeed been seen to send down an opponent in such and such a location, which would hopefully lead to confirmation of another kill. It was all the more important during a land battle where opponents might come down between the lines, where the wreck was not so available to inspect and verify.

During April 1917 *Jasta* 11 amassed a total of 89 victories, its nearest rivals being *Jasta* 5 with 32 and *Jasta* 12 with 23 (*Jasta* 2 came fourth with 21). Altogether, the German fighter pilots claimed almost 300 Allied air-

The von Richthofen brothers, Manfred and Lothar, both decorated with the *Pour le Mérite*

Kurt Wolff of *Jasta* 11 won the *Blue Max* with this unit whilst serving under Manfred von Richthofen. He claimed 33 victories, all but two of which were scored with *Jasta* 11. Wolff's final two kills were claimed during his time as CO of *Jasta* 29. He was killed in action on 15 September 1917 in one of the new Fokker Triplanes, shot down by Norman McGregor of 10 Naval Squadron

craft and balloons. *Jasta* 11 also topped the individual pilot claims, with Wolff achieving 22 victories, von Richthofen and Schäfer 21 each and Lothar von Richthofen 15 – Festner was eighth on the list with ten. He might well have scored more, but on 25 April he became the unit's only casualty of the month, shot down attacking BE 2s in Albatros D III D.2251/16. Nevertheless, 89 for 1 was an amazing score.

The Baron himself downed no fewer than four British aeroplanes on 29 April. His father had arrived at the airfield that day on a visit while his two sons were in the air. The Rittmeister later wrote;

'My brother was the first to climb from his machine, and he greeted the old gentleman with the words, "Good day, father. I have just shot down an Englishman". Immediately after, I also climbed out of my machine and greeted him, "Good day, father. I have just shot down an Englishman". The old gentleman felt very happy, and he was delighted.

'Towards midday we flew once more. This time I was again lucky and shot down my second Englishman of the day. After the midday dinner I slept a little. I was again quite fresh. Wolff had fought the enemy in the meantime with his group of machines, and had himself bagged an enemy; Schäfer had also beaten one. In the afternoon my brother and I, accompanied by Schäfer and Allmenröder, flew twice more.

'The first afternoon flight was a failure. The second was all the better. Soon after we had come to the lines a hostile squadron met us. Unfortunately they were at a higher altitude, so we could not do anything. We tried to climb to their level, but did not succeed. We had to let them go.

'We flew along the lines, my brother next to me in front of the others. Suddenly, I noticed two hostile artillery fliers approaching

33

our front in the most impertinent and provocative manner. I waved to my brother and he understood my meaning. We flew side by side, increasing our speed. Each of us felt certain that he was superior to the enemy. It was a great thing that we could absolutely rely on one another.

'My brother was the first to approach his enemy. He attacked the first and I took care of the second. At the last moment I quickly looked round in order to feel sure that there was no third aeroplane about but we were alone. Soon I had got on the favourable side of my opponent. A short spell of quick firing and the enemy machine went to pieces. I never had a more rapid success.

'While I was still looking where my enemy's fragments were falling, I noticed my brother, scarcely 500 yards away, was still fighting his opponent.

'I had time to study the struggle and must say that I could not have done any better than he did. Suddenly, the machine reared, a certain indication that the pilot had been hit. The machine fell and the planes of the enemy apparatus went to pieces, falling quite close to my victim. I flew towards my brother and we congratulated one another by waving.'

The *Jasta* pilots then spotted a formation of SPADs and Sopwith Triplanes, but they did not seem too intent on taking on the German fighters immediately. A short while later, however, battle was joined. Von Richthofen continued;

'My opponent had a very good and very fast machine. However, he did not succeed in reaching the English lines. I began to fire at him when we were above Lens. I started shooting when I was much too far away, but that was merely a trick of mine, for I not so much wanted to hit him as frighten him. I succeeded and caught him up. He began to fly round with me and I gradually edged in closer and closer.

'Finally, when almost touching him, I aimed very carefully from 50 yards. I heard a slight hissing noise, a sure sign that petrol tanks had been hit. Then I saw a bright flame and my lord (a name given to Englishmen by German fighter pilots) disappeared below me. This was my fourth victim of the day.'

Von Richthofen had shot down a SPAD VII, a FE 2d, a BE 2e and a Sopwith Triplane, whilst his brother Lothar had also claimed a SPAD VII and a BE two-seater.

The handful of *Jasta* 11 pilots continued to score heavily during May, with a further 30 victories, but they also had another pilot killed, and Lothar and Allmenröder were wounded – the former whilst flying D III D.776/17 on the 13th, and the latter, amazingly, in the same machine 12 days later. On a more positive note, yet another future *Jasta* 11 ace had enjoyed success during this period, Eberhardt Mohnicke, who joined the unit on the last day of April, arriving with one kill from KG 2. He had downed a further six British machines by the late summer.

Fellow *Jasta* 11 ace Karl Allmenröder enjoyed many successes with the unit between February and June 1917, amassing 30 kills. A great tactician, he was always prepared to try something new in combat, as the following combat report by FE 8 pilot, 2Lt R E Neve, of No 40 Sqn shows;

'FE 8 (pilots) saw 2 H.A. east of Annoeulin. Three H.A., who appeared to be working with these two, dived from above and attacked (our) formation.

'(Neve) was engaged with several H.A. for about 5 minutes when gun jammed. One H.A. apparently noticed that FE 8's gun was out of action and fired a burst from right hand rear, and throttled down to FE 8's speed.

'FE 8 pilot was then wounded and had great difficulty in breathing – a bullet also grazed his head which was apparently sheared off by the helmet. Petrol tank was then pierced and engine stopped – FE 8 feigned to land in hostile territory. At 500 ft FE 8 (pilot) tried gravity tank, engine re-started, and FE 8 managed to cross the lines at 80 mph.

'FE 8 pilot becoming faint decided to land as soon as possible, and seeing three soldiers endeavoured to land near them. Owing to aileron being shot away, FE 8 made a bad landing, turned over and caught fire. Pilot scrambled out with coat and gloves ablaze. He rolled over on the ground and soldiers took off their coats and smothered fire, afterwards carrying him to a place of safety. The machine was then shelled.'

This action had taken place on 9 March, and had resulted in Allmenröder claiming only his second kill, and 2Lt R E Neve effecting a lucky escape. As the combat report shows, it seemed to the FE 8 pilots that two Albatros Scouts were acting as decoys for a second group of fighters flying above them.

Neve's successful evading action led Allmenröder to claim that the FE 8 had come down inside German lines, and despite the British aircraft making it back to Allied territory, German artillery batteries confirmed the *Jagdflieger's* success prior to destroying the damaged fighter with a well-placed barrage. A further three FE 8s from No 40 Sqn were also brought down by pilots from *Jasta* 11 inside German lines during this engagement, two being credited to Karl Schäfer and the third to Kurt Wolff.

Soon after the unit had taken delivery of its first Albatros D Vs, the Baron was shot down and wounded on 6 July in a fight with FE 2s of No 20 Sqn, although he managed to force-land his damaged D V near La Montagne, south of Wervicq-Sud. This action came shortly after he had been chosen to lead the first *Jagdgeschwader* Nr. I (JG I), formed in June, which was comprised of the four *Jastas* referred to earlier – 4, 6, 10 and 11.

In the meantime, Karl Allmenröder had been killed on 27 June, and Kurt Wolff had been promoted to lead the *Jasta* following von Richthofen's assignment to JG I. The new commander lasted just a matter of weeks in the job, however, for he was wounded on 11 July, having scored 31 victories. Willy Reinhard then led *Jasta* 11 until he too was wounded at the beginning of September.

In the autumn the Fokker Dr I began to arrive in small numbers, and soon JG I had enough Triplanes on strength to fly them on a regular basis. It remained the unit's staple fighter, except for a brief period during the winter of 1917-18, until the arrival of the Fokker D VII in the early summer of 1918.

JASTA 12 TO *JASTA* 16

Jasta 12 was yet another unit that boasted many excellent pilots, and it was initially led by Paul von Osterroht (seven victories) until he was killed on 23 April. His successor was Oblt Adolf Ritter von Tutschek, a Bavarian nearing his 26th birthday. A former infantry officer on both the Western and Eastern Fronts, he had been highly decorated as a soldier, and knighted (Ritter) even before becoming a pilot. Via two-seaters, he joined *Jasta* 2, where he scored three victories before taking command of *Jasta* 12.

On 20 May 1917 von Tutschek claimed his tenth victory in the shape of a SPAD VII from No 23 Sqn. He later described the action in a letter;

'Further back was another aircraft, which I assumed was a D II coming to visit us. I put the stick between my knees and hummed a melody and sat on my rather stiff hands as my Albatros glided quietly down. I was over the airstrip when all at once two machine guns began to rattle. Although I felt I wasn't the target, I instinctively pulled my crate and gave it gas. I couldn't believe my eyes when I saw that the supposed D II was a very impudent SPAD single-seater. He had taken on my good, unsuspecting (Vfw) Schorisch, who was going down in steep spirals with the Englishman right behind him with his gun blazing.

'At several hundred metres I opened fire on this impudent patron in order to relieve my comrade of his pursuer. Sure enough, he banked towards me. He obviously thought it would be a sporting accomplishment to shoot down both "Boche Bunnies" over their own airfield. But he had imagined his task too simple. Schorisch was down too low to be able to help me and we remained alone. Three or four times we passed each other, firing short bursts of machine gun fire head on, then I sat over and behind him. Ten shots from me and the SPAD reared up vertically. I pulled up my bird to avoid ramming him, and for an instant I am directly over him. From beneath, his machine gun rattles upward and wood splinters fly from my fuselage. He tumbles and begins to plunge. I am behind. He is done, I think, but he takes control of his machine and heads for the lines in a dive.

'I chase after him and again my machine guns speak. He turns a half loop over his left wing and heads toward me, his wheels up and shooting. Afterwards he slides off, catches himself and climbs. He must be a bigshot, I think. I succeed in coming close behind him but again the same manoeuvre as before. Close under me he races by and I see his light brown coat as he raises his arm in a threat. Suddenly something hits me in the head. I can't imagine what. As I look in my sights, my right gun won't fire. To aim over the left gun is impractical and for the novice, uncomfortable . . . but it worked. In the meantime my SPAD is lower, and thanks to his able flying, has pulled closer to his lines. He winds, somersaults but never again can I get him properly, or long enough before my gun.

Ulrich Neckel flew with *Jasta* 12 in 1917-18 and gained at least ten victories with this unit before moving firstly to *Jasta* 13, then *Jasta* 19 and finally *Jasta* 6, where he served as its CO. Neckel ended the war with 30 victories and the *Blue Max*

Jasta 12 lined up on Toulis airfield on 15 March 1918, by which time it was operating a mix of Albatros Scouts and Fokker Triplanes. The unit was in transition from the D V to the Triplane when this photograph was taken. Like most other pilots of the *Jasta*, Ulrich Neckel had one of each type of fighter at his disposal during this period, both marked with his white arrowhead on the fuselage. *Jasta* 12's unit marking was a black tail and rear fuselage and white nose. Neckel's two machines can be seen in the foreground, clearly showing the personal emblems and white noses of both the Albatros and the Fokker (*G VanWyngarden collection*)

'Again I sit behind him and again he climbs and flips into a bank. I cut the bank, fire my gun and almost ram him. A tiny flame under the seat and a moment later a bright red flame engulfs the Englishman. One shot had hit the fuel tank. The SPAD flies a few hundred metres then it goes into a dive, trailing black smoke from an altitude of 700 metres. After impact with the ground a bright red flame consumes what is left of the enemy aircraft, which crashes four kilometres behind our lines near Riencourt.'

By August von Tutschek had achieved a total of 23 kills, and been awarded the *Blue Max*. However, he was also seriously wounded by Royal Naval Air Service ace C D Booker, of 8 Naval Squadron, that same month. After a long recuperation, von Tutschek returned to the front to lead JG II, and he was subsequently killed flying a Dr I with the unit in March 1918.

Ltn Adolf Schulte was *Jasta* 12's first ace, having joined the unit in November 1916. During the early months of 1917, he succeeded in destroying eight aircraft, but became an early casualty of the Battle of Arras. On 12 April 1917 he collided with an FE 2d from No 18 Sqn whilst flying Albatros D III D.1996/16 – all three men died. Another pilot who scored nine kills in 1917 was Reinhold Jörke, who would go on to raise his tally to 14 flying with other units by war's end. Finally, Friedrich Gille also scored six victories in 1917.

The distinction of scoring *Jasta* 12's 100th victory fell to ace Viktor Schobinger on 21 October 1917. A former machine gunner who left the trenches to become a pilot, he spent time flying two-seaters prior to joining the *Jasta*. Schobinger participated in the dogfight that saw his CO, von Tutschek, badly wounded, and succeeded in downing C D Booker of 8 Naval Squadron moments after he had despatched the *Staffelführer*. Like the latter, the British pilot also survived the encounter, but he may well have been prevented from finishing von Tutschek off by Schobinger's timely action. With a total of eight victories, Viktor Schobinger managed to survive his time in the frontline and spend the rest of the war as an instructor.

Another of *Jasta* 12's aces from 1917 was Ulrich Neckel, who finished the war with 30 victories. A former artillery man turned flyer, he arrived at the unit having gained experience with two-seaters, prior to joining *Jasta* 12 in September 1917. By the end of that same month he had gained two victories, and come the spring of 1918, Neckel's score had risen to ten. He then left *Jasta* 12 for *Jasta* 13. During his time with the former unit, Neckel had the rare distinction of having either an Albatros or a Triplane to fly, both of which were adorned with his white chevron marking on the fuselage. From late 1917 through to early 1918, *Jasta* 12 used both types as part of JG II under von Tutschek, the *Jagdgeschwader* being comprised of *Jastas* 12, 13, 15 and 19.

Before his period with *Jasta* 7, Paul Billik had flown with *Jasta* 12 in early 1917, flying this Albatros D V marked with a large black swastika on a white square. As seen in the photograph reproduced on page 26, Hermann Kunz of *Jasta* 7 also marked his aircraft with a swastika, having perhaps been influenced to adopt the good luck symbol following the arrival of Billik on *Jasta* 12. The latter pilot went on to score a total of 31 victories, mostly as commander of *Jasta* 52 in 1918

Rudolf Berthold is seen in the cockpit of his Albatros D II D.1717/16 at Bühl airfield whilst serving with *Jasta* 14. The aircraft has bears no specific markings other than the ply fuselage was probably stained a reddish brown colour. Note the fuselage radiators which caused drag and were mounted on the wing in later models of the Albatros
(*G VanWyngarden collection*)

Paul Billik enjoyed his first successes with *Jasta* 12 in the spring of 1917, scoring four victories, followed by four more with *Jasta* 7. In 1918 he commanded *Jasta* 52, ending the war with 31 kills. Billik also ended the conflict as a prisoner of war, having been shot down behind Allied lines on 10 August. Despite his high score, his capture effectively put paid to him receiving the *Blue Max*.

Jasta 14 had several successful pilots pass through its ranks during 1917, including Joseph Veltjens (at least 10 of his 35 victories were scored flying Albatros Scouts) and Berthold. With five confirmed and one

Albatros D IIIs of *Jasta* 14 in the spring of 1917. They are, from right to left, Friedrich Vonschott's aircraft with unusual 'star' marking, Berthold's 'winged sword' D III, (the third scout is devoid of a personal marking) and Josef Veltjen's white Indian arrow-marked machine
(*HAC/UTD via G VanWyngarden*)

Kurt Monnington used this unusually camouflaged Albatros D V during his time with *Jasta* 15. It carried this grim skull and crossbones motif on a white fuselage band. The significance of the marking remains unclear, for Monnington did not belong to any 'Death's Head Hussar' Regiment – he probably just liked the emblem! Monnington later became an ace flying Fokker fighters
(*P Grosz via G VanWyngarden*)

Georg von Hantelmann's aircraft bore a skull and crossbones marking similar in style to that used by Monnington. In von Hantelmann's case, however, the insignia indicated his prior service with the Braunschweiger Hussar Regiment Nr.17, whose men wore a 'death's head' cap badge. Here, the pilot is seen seated on his Albatros D V, which also had a dark blue fuselage and red nose area, thus denoting its operation by *Jasta* 15. Finally, the fighter's wings and rudder were covered in lozenge fabric (*G VanWyngarden collection*)

Line up of *Jasta* 15 machines. They are, from the right, Heinrich Gontermann's mottled D V with red fuselage band, (the pilot for the second scout remains unknown, although the aircraft has a mottled finish and a white fuselage band), Monnington's 'death's head' D V and Haussmann's D.2042/17 (*G VanWyngarden collection*)

unconfirmed kills, Hans Bowski also became an ace with the unit in that same year, prior to being wounded on 3 September. He later joined *Jasta* 51, but failed to add to his score.

Following Rudolf Berthold's elevation to the position of CO of JG II in March 1918 after the loss of von Tutschek, the former wanted his old unit, *Jasta* 18, to be a part of his new command. However, the only way he could achieve this was to exchange the pilots of this *Jasta* with those of *Jasta* 15. On the face of it, this seems a rather extreme measure, but it happened, and the mass exchange of pilots took place while keeping the four numbered *Jastas* intact! Again, we have already mentioned several of the successful pilots that were a part of the old *Jasta* 15 when they were with other units, and as both *Jastas* flew Albatros and Fokker Triplanes, it is not easy to tell who flew what, and when. However, it can be said with authority that Ernst Udet certainly gained victories two to six with *Jasta* 15, prior to going to *Jasta* 37 in August 1917.

Royal Bavarian *Jasta* 16 had Ludwig Hanstein as its first ace, gaining his second to eleventh victories between March and October 1917, after which time he moved to *Jasta* 35. Despite being a Prussian, Hanstein saw most of his active service in Bavarian units, and this included flying a Fokker D II with FA 9 on 12 October 1916 – the day on which he forced an RNAS Sopwith 1½ Strutter down on Frieburg airfield during an

Oliver Freiherr von Beaulieu-Marconnay, who scored 25 victories in World War 1, began his fighting career with *Jasta* 15 and gained his first kills with the Albatros. His aircraft was marked with the branding iron insignia of his 4th Prussian Dragoon Regiment, and he later used the same marking on his D VIIs. He died of wounds on 16 October 1918, aged 20, but was awarded the *Blue Max* shortly before he passed away

D IIs (LVG-built) of *Jasta* 16b. On the left is the scout flown by Robert Dycke (two victories), marked with the Bavarian crest in a white diamond. The pilot of the second fighter remains unknown, but with the horseshoe motif upside-down, did his luck 'run out'?! The third D II is Ludwig Hanstein's diamond-marked machine – note that this aircraft is the only one that still has large white squares beneath its wing crosses. The last machine bears a white comet insignia, which was just one of the many variations of a flaming comet used on numerous German aircraft in World War 1. Note too the airman working on the hanger roof
(*G VanWyngarden collection*)

Theodor Rumpel's zebra-striped Albatros D V of *Jasta* 16b. Rumpel scored two kills with the *Jasta* before going to *Jasta* 23 to become an ace on 18 February 1918. He was severely wounded on 24 March
(*Carlson/Connors/via G VanWyngarden*)

Allied raid on Oldendorf. *Jasta* 16b operated mainly on the French front, but when Hanstein took command of *Jasta* 35 at the end of 1917, he was just as successful against the British. After almost two solid years in the frontline, he eventually fell to a Bristol Fighter from No 11 Sqn on 21 March 1918, moments after recording his 16 kill.

Karl Schattauer scored his first victory with *Jasta* 23b, and like Hanstein, it did not seem to matter at this stage that he was a Prussian, even when he moved to *Jasta* 16b in September. On 27 May 1918, by which time he had scored nine victories and was operating on the British front, Schattauer was so badly wounded that he never saw action again.

For much of the time that Karl Schattauer was with *Jasta* 16b, the unit's CO was Heinrich Geigl. The latter had arrived at the *Jasta* on

Ltn Theodor Rumpel of Jasta 16b

17 August 1917, having already scored six kills with *Jasta* 34. A Bavarian, he downed his seventh aircraft three days later, and by the spring of 1918 his score had risen to 12. Geigl was killed soon afterwards, his fighter colliding with a Sopwith Camel from No 65 Sqn. The British fighter was credited as being his 13th, and last, victory.

A pre-war aviator, Karl Odebrett had seen action on the Russian Front in 1915 prior to moving to *Jasta* 16 in France late the following year. Having brought one victory with him from the east, he scored a further six before being slightly wounded in September 1917 by AA fire. In December Odebrett took command of the newly-formed *Jasta* 42, and by war's end he had claimed 21 victories. He died from liver failure in February 1930, aged 39.

Friedrich (Fritz) Ritter von Röth had been with *Jasta* 23 at the beginning of 1918, having previously served in the artillery. Wounded and

Jasta 16b's airfield. At far right is Rumpel's striped machine, and parked alongside it is one of Otto Kissenberth's edelweiss-marked black Albatros D Vs (*G VanWyngarden collection*)

having spent a year in hospital, he joined the flying service and, via two-seaters, became a fighter pilot. von Röth succumbed to the anti-balloon bug from the start of 1918, to the extent that only one of his first ten kills was an aeroplane. Moving to *Jasta* 16 later in 1918, he ended the war with 28 victories, 20 of which were balloons. This made von Röth the highest scoring German pilot against these dangerous targets. Most of his attacks were carefully planned, as Carl Degelow, an ace with *Jasta* 7 and then *Jasta* 40, related;

'In attempting to shoot down captive balloons, wind conditions are of great importance. This was ably demonstrated by Oblt Fritz Ritter von Röth, our greatest balloon-busting ace.

Whilst leading *Jasta* 35b, Ludwig Hanstein used this Albatros D V, which featured a large six-pointed star on the fuselage. Before his death on 31 March 1918, he had scored 16 kills. Hanstein was shot down in combat with a Bristol Fighter from No 11 Sqn. Note the rear view mirrors and telescopic gun sight

Friedrich 'Fritz' Ritter von Röth led *Jasta* 16b following service with *Jasta* 23b. He is leaning on an Albatros D Va that features the black tail unit of *Jasta* 16b, as well as a coloured fuselage band as his personal insignia. Note the anemometer-type airspeed indicator (ASI) and auxiliary strut above and behind von Röth's right arm (*G VanWyngarden collection*)

This OAW-built Albatros D Va was flown by the Bavarian 'balloon-buster' Fritz Ritter von Röth of *Jasta* 23b in early 1918. The black and white fuselage disc was his personal marking, while the white band wrapped vertically around the tail surfaces was the unit marking. Wings, tailplane and rudder were probably covered in lozenge fabric, while most of the fuselage remained clear varnished plywood. The spinner was probably white. If the individual in the cockpit is indeed Röth, it is either a very cold day or he is merely suited-up for the camera, for the machine is obviously not about to take off, with the engine cowling still absent and the ladder propped up against the fuselage (*G VanWyngarden collection*)

Otto Kissenberth also flew an edel-weiss-marked Albatros D V (D.2263/17) when he assumed command of *Jasta* 23b in the summer of 1917. On this occasion his aircraft was totally black except for his personal emblem, with the serial number – minus the '/17' – in white. The scout's wings are covered in five-coloured lozenge fabric. Note the anemometer type ASI on the interplane strut (*G VanWyngarden collection*)

Otto Kissenberth flew with *Kek* Enisheim prior to service with *Jasta* 16b, with whom he brought his score to six. He then commanded *Jasta* 23b. Despite wearing eye-glasses, Kissenberth had scored 20 kills by the time he was injured in a crash whilst flying a captured Sopwith Camel on 19 May 1918

'Before every attack, he spent hours on end peering through a telescope, watching the manoeuvres of the aeroplanes protecting his intended target. Most important of all, he devoted considerable time to the weather prediction charts. He would wait for a favourable day on which the wind was somewhat parallel to the front and to the row of balloons. Then he would go up to a very high altitude and dive straight down on the carefully arranged row of British gas-bags. By this tactic, von Röth achieved, first of all, a quick and almost unnoticed approach to the balloons. Secondly, the speed of his single-seat fighter, aided by the speed of the wind, enabled him to fly so fast through the curtain of protective anti-aircraft and machine gun fire that he was too fast-moving a target to hit.'

Fellow *Jasta* 16b ace Otto Kissenberth's story is worthy of a book on its own. A native of Bavaria, he was born in February 1893 and studied in France, before completing an engineering degree in Münich. Kissenberth then began working in an aircraft company, before entering military aviation upon the outbreak of war. Wounded whilst flying two-seaters, he returned to become a fighter pilot with *Kek* Einsisheim, and in his first real combat shot down three raiding bombers on 12 October 1916. By the late spring of 1917 Kissenberth had moved to *Jasta* 16b, were he scored his next three victories, before transferring to *Jasta* 23b. By the end of the year he had 18 kills to his name, and had been made commander of his unit.

Early in 1918 Kissenberth raised his tally to 20, but was then badly injured flying a captured Sopwith Camel. He received the *Pour le Mérite* in June 1918, but was never considered fit enough to return to the front. Having survived the war, Kissenberth died in a mountain fall in the Bavarian Alps in August 1919.

Kissenberth's black-fuselaged Albatros D V in *Jasta* 16b. The edelweiss emblem is in white, with yellow stamens, the rudder is clear-doped and the upper wings and tailplane green and mauve (*P Grosz via G VanWyngarden*)

THE FIGHTER GROUPS

Despite the formation of JG I in June 1917, no other large – *permanent* – *Jasta* groupings were made until 2 February 1918, at which time JGs II and III were created under the command of Adolf Ritter von Tutschek and Bruno Loerzer respectively.

However, the idea of groups had first been considered as early as April 1917 with the creation of a 6th Army *Jagdgruppe,* commanded by Manfred von Richthofen, comprising *Jastas* 3, 4, 11 and 33. Note that these were not the same four units which, in June of that year, became JG I. In the main, the first *Jagdgruppe* existed essentially for the administration purposes of the German 6th Army Sector. It did not mean that the four units flew together regularly as one large formation, although von Richthofen was able to plan, to some extent, operations over the sector he was responsible for, and overlap patrol areas as necessary.

It has to be remembered that formation flying in World War 1 was not something that could be organised very well. There were no radio aids, and in the often dull and cloudy conditions which prevailed over northern France, groups of aircraft could soon be lost to view. Nor were leaders always able to keep visual and mental track of a large number of aeroplanes. Von Richthofen himself was known to be able to do this better than most, but once a full-blooded combat developed, it was difficult to keep tabs on everyone . . . and stay alive. The only means of signalling was by pistol flare to indicate a few orders – enemy in sight, reform on me, go home, etc.

By mid-1917 the colours and individual markings of pilots' machines had become well established, and in this way a leader could quickly and easily pick out one of his men. If it looked as if the pilot was up against some stiff opposition, but the markings indicated it was an experienced flyer in the cockpit, help need not perhaps be deemed essential. On the other hand, if the markings indicated a new or inexperienced man, help might be needed sooner rather than later. With pilots also keen to have their victory claims verified on the ground, it was thought much easier for the soldiery to be able to confirm that such-and-such a coloured machine, or one marked with a specific symbol or letter, had been seen to despatch the Allied machine or balloon in question.

To all intents and purposes, the Baron continued to lead his own *Jasta* 11, but had command control over the other three units too, although most daily sorties were still led and planned by each *Staffelführer*, unless there was some major offensive in being.

The non-permanent *Jagdgruppen* later became more familiar, and by the autumn of 1917 several had been formed, but mostly for just limited periods so as to co-operate with a ground battle or offensive. Some became known by a number, whilst others adopted the name of their leader or area, such as *Jagdgruppe Lille* or *Jagdgruppe* 'Tutscheck'. Some of them were not long-lived – *Jagdgruppe* 'Tutscheck', for example, comprising *Jastas* 12, 30 and 37, only existed between 4 and 11 August 1917.

German aces could and did command these groups, while others were led by senior – regular – commanders. Once JG I was formed, which was a permanent grouping, von Richthofen, as its first leader, not only controlled its operations, but also the replacement leaders and, to a degree, those pilots who would remain and those who would not.

This formation, and those which followed (JGs II, III and finally IV, in October 1918, with Eduard Ritter von Schleich commanding), became known on the Allied side as 'Circuses'. This was because these *Jagdgeschwaderen* moved from sector to sector, depending on where they were needed, and in part because of the highly decorated machines they flew. However, most *Jastas* possessed highly decorated aeroplanes, so it was more likely that the sobriquet was derived from the former trait rather than the latter.

Of course, it was natural for Allied units to believe that they were always up against the von Richthofen 'Circus', or another 'Circus', if some of the machines were coloured red, or just highly decorated. It gave them some kudos, and if they had lost a couple of men, some excuse. Often one reads in combat reports of a flight of, say, SE 5as meeting 50 or more German fighters, appearing to indicate a whole group, but more often than not it was just exaggeration, or they 'felt' that there had been over 50. *Jasta* numbers were much smaller, although other nearby *Jastas*, seeing action taking place, would often join in to make a hard-pressed Allied unit appear as if it was under attack from a veritable mass of German fighters.

By the end of 1916, almost 30 *Jastas* had been formed, with all but *Jasta* 25, which operated on the Macedonian Front, operating in France – note that *Jastas* 1, 31 and 39 experienced a brief period of action in Italy, whilst *Jasta* 55 operated in Palestine.

Some of these units were to become quite famous due to their claims, and ace pilots, whilst others have remained in relative obscurity. Those on the northern, British, part of the frontline tended to see more combat than those on the southern, French, sectors, and the impression is that the more experienced units and pilots fought against the RFC/RAF and RNAS. However, some successful pilots ran up respectable scores against the French, and remained operating on the French front till war's end.

As is well known, von Richthofen and his pilots fought on the British Front almost exclusively, and only came upon French machines where the British and French sectors linked up.

JASTA 17 ONWARDS

Jasta 17 operated on the French front in its early days. Its top ace, Julius Buckler, began scoring against French aircraft in December 1916, and he became an ace in April 1917. The unit then moved to the British front, where Buckler continued to add to his tally. A former infantryman, he had started working life as a roofer pre-war, planned to be an architect, and had ended up working for Anthony Fokker, the famous Dutch aircraft designer. By November 1917 he had run his score to 30, but was then badly wounded. Buckler received the *Pour le Mérite*, and returned to *Jasta* 17 in the spring of 1918.

During the latter half of 1917 Buckler often had two aircraft at his disposal so that he was always able to fly – these fighters were named *Lilly* and *Mops*. He later wrote about his numerous engagements, with the following account being typical of the action he experienced during 1917-18;

'From the aerodrome came a report, "Enemy flyer over Bruges". As everyone was sleeping I went alone to the airfield, mounted my *Mops* with just shirt, trousers, scarf and goggles on, and flew towards the old Flanders town.

'There was lightning and the raindrops stung my face like needles. At 200 metres I plunged into the clouds, saw a hole, pushed through, came into the clouds again, climbed even higher and finally at 3200 metres height, had a blue sky and luminous sunshine above me.

Ace pilots with *Jasta* 18. Sitting in the front row, from left to right, are Paul Strähle (15 kills), Josef Veltjens (35 kills), unit CO Rudolf Berthold (44 kills), Harold Auffarth (30 kills) and Otto Schober. Standing at the rear, again from left to right, are Hugo Schäfer (11 kills), Richard Runge (8 kills), Ernst Turck (1 kill), Walter Dingel (2 kills) and Arthur Rahn (6 kills)

Hugo Schäfer poses for the camera in his snake/serpent-marked Albatros D V whilst with *Jasta* 18. He brought this machine with him during the pilot exchange with *Jasta* 15, and it had the standard unit colours of a red nose and blue fuselage (*P Grosz via G VanWyngarden*)

Josef Veltjens continued to have his aircraft marked with the winged arrow design seen here, this Albatros D V photo having probably been taken in February 1918 while he was still a member of *Jasta* 18. Thus, aside from his personal white arrow marking, the fighter had a red nose and blue fuselage (*G VanWyngarden collection*)

Veltjens in the cockpit of his Albatros D V. Note the rear view mirror and telescopic sight. He flew with *Jastas* 14, 18 and 15, and had scored 35 victories by the end of the war (*G VanWyngarden collection*)

'A tightly-closed white sea of cloud cut me off from the earth. It was so beautiful to fly up here in the sunshine over the peacefully slumbering clouds that I forgot entirely about the war. In this solitude I met an enemy flyer.

'He came from the direction of Bruges and was obviously in the act of flying home. He was flying about 200 metres higher than I. I followed him, pushed my *Mops* to 2000 revs, pulled it up and shot from below.

'He wheeled round immediately, which is what I wanted. I played the runaway. He pounced behind me and then I made a sudden turn. He sped past me and, sitting on his neck, I gave him a couple of well-aimed bursts from 15 to 20 metres distance. His machine emitted smoke then burst into flames.

'I saw the inmate stand up. He did not want to burn, the brave man, preferring to jump to his death from 3000 metres rather than a fiery death. I cannot describe what went on within me when I saw this person plunging into the depths before my eyes, followed by his burning machine.'

Wounded again on 6 May – his fifth wound of the war – with his score at 33, Buckler did not return until the autumn, adding his last three kills during October. He died in Berlin in 1960.

Buckler's is a case in point that he was the *Jasta* star, increasing his score steadily while other pilots claimed the odd one or two here and there. For example, during the period between 29 September and 29 November he scored 17 victories, while one other pilot added just one to the *Jasta* tally. And most of this time Buckler was still only a Vizefeldwebel (senior NCO), not being commissioned until 18 November 1917. This, of course, was the system encouraged by the Germans, where the unit would support the man who had the skill to perform well.

This sort of thing led people to believe that an ace such as von Richthofen hogged all the combat, or only scored because he was protected by his men, or pulled rank and had others' victories added to his own score. This was all nonsense. He was good, and the German *Jasta* system worked. In a free-for-all fight their might be no claims, whereas in a measured attack by a proven leader or star performer, kills were more certain. And that was the object – to shoot down the aircraft of one's enemy.

Georg Strasser was the only other scorer of note within *Jasta* 17 in 1916-17, downing seven opponents before being badly wounded in December. He too was a Vizefeldwebel.

This axe-marked D V (D.4594/17) was flown by Paul Strähle. While he used this aircraft with *Jasta* 18, this photograph was taken in late 1917 following his move to *Jasta* 57. The fighter is seen heading a line up of other Albatros Scouts at Boistrancourt airfield

Albatros D II flown by Ltn Wilhelm Leusch of *Jasta* 19, circa April 1917. The pilot's personal marking consisted of a black 'L' with white outline in the characteristic style of this *Jasta* at this time. Leusch later commanded the *Jasta*, ending the war with five victories. Note the Windhoff radiator below the fuselage struts (*G VanWyngarden collection*)

Jasta 18 was partly covered earlier in dealing with the big pilot swap it carried out with *Jasta* 15 due to Rudolf Berthold's promotion. Between 14 April 1917 and 2 October, Berthold increased his score to 28 whilst flying an Albatros and, perhaps, a Pfalz D III – 14 of these kills were claimed in September alone. Like Buckler in *Jasta* 17, Berthold was known for his series of wounds and injuries, but these never kept him away from the battlefront for very long. Shot down on one occasion, he suffered a fractured skull, broken nose, pelvis and thigh. Indeed, injury finally caused him to leave *Jasta* 18 when he suffered a smashed right upper arm in combat in October 1917. Upon his return to command JG II in February 1918, Berthold's injured arm was still virtually useless, yet he enjoyed further success in combat.

Richard Runge, from Hamburg, claimed seven of his eight victories with *Jasta* 18 in 1917, before being shot down in flames by Lt K B Montgomery of No 45 Sqn just a week before his 27th birthday. Another Albatros ace from this same year was Ernst Wiessner from Stuttgart. He fell to a No 20 Sqn FE 2 crew on 7 June after having scored five victories, with another unconfirmed.

Erich Hahn took command of *Jasta* 19 in November 1916 after gaining one victory with *Jasta* 1. Leading his new unit, he downed three French machines and two balloons in April 1917, one of which was a SPAD VII flown by the French ace René Doumer, on the 26th. However, on 4 September 1917 he himself fell to another French ace in Georges Madon of Spa 38, becoming the latter's 16th kill. Hahn had been the first *Jasta* pilot to receive the Knight's Cross of the Saxon Military St Henry Order.

Three pilots from *Jasta* 21 – Ltn Keller, Karl Schmuckle (six victories) and Karl Thom. The latter scored 14 victories in 1917, and in 1918 added another 13 to his tally. A severe wound eventually put him out of the war, but he did receive the *Pour le Mérite* shortly before the Armistice

Ernst Hess commanded *Jasta* 19 from 18 September 1917, joining the unit from *Jasta* 28, where he had brought his score to 14. Gaining three more kills, he was shot down in Albatros D Va 5347/17 on 23 December, his death being attributed to Adjudant De Kergolay of N96 – this was the Frenchman's first success. Thus it can be seen that experience cannot out-run luck.

Walter Böning, who would end his war on 30 May 1918 with *Jasta* 76, and with 17 kills, scored his first six victories with *Jasta* 19. A former Bavarian infantryman, he had flown two-seaters with FA6b prior to becoming a fighter pilot. Assigned to *Jasta* 19, he downed two French air-craft and a balloon in April 1917, then four more French machines by the end of the year.

Saxon *Jagdstaffel* 21 had some big names amongst its pilots. Karl Thom was a pre-war soldier and was decorated – and wounded – in the early weeks of the war. Once an aviator, he served in two-seaters in the Vosges and then in Rumania. Shot down and captured whilst flying in the latter region, he managed to effect an escape, which would subsequently be bad news for many Allied airmen over the Western Front. An NCO when he

Karl Thom flew Albatros D V D.2164/17 whilst with *Jasta* 21. It bears both the unit marking of a black and white fuselage band and his personal emblem in the shape of a white 'T'. Note too the small black '5' between the fuselage cross and the tail, and a head-rest. It is possible that this machine was also flown by fellow ace Ltn Emil Thuy, who scored 13 of his eventual 35 victories during his time with *Jasta* 21

Alfred Lenz flew this interestingly-marked Albatros D V (D.2030/17) with *Jasta* 22. Apart from his personal emblem of a band of white diamonds round the fuselage, there is a witch(?) on a bird (duck?) which has a coloured beak (red, orange or yellow), looking through a telescope at what appears to be a DH 2 fighter. Lenz was a Bavarian, so it may be that the fuselage was cobalt blue rather than green, and there is no fuselage cross. Upper wings were mauve and green, undersides sky blue. Underwing crosses were not edged in white, and struts were grey. Despite flying Fokkers in 1915, and scoring one victory, Lenz did not score again (with either *Jasta* 4 or 14) until he served as leader of *Jasta* 22 in 1918. He ended the war with six victories

The German ace Eduard Ritter von Schleich – the 'Black Knight' – initially flew this well known Albatros D V with *Jasta* 21. Its fuselage is two-tone coloured, and a black and white fuselage band is worn immediately behind the cockpit. Finally, a Bavarian lion adorns a blue and white diamond-coloured circle (*G VanWyngarden collection*)

was assigned to *Jasta* 21, Thom had achieved 14 victories by the end of 1917 on the French front, but was wounded in a balloon attack on 23 December. By 4 August his score had risen to 27 victories (all bar four of these kills were against the French), and although he had also won the *Pour le Mérite*, he was not commissioned until 11 August 1918. All of Thom's aircraft carried a large 'T' on their fuselage.

Bavarian Eduard Ritter von Schleich accounted for 35 French and British aeroplanes and one balloon in the war, and he too won the coveted *Blue Max*. Born in Munich, he was known as the 'Black Knight' due to the colour of his aircraft. Older than many pilots (he was 26 when the war began), von Schleich had previously served as an infantrymen pre-war, being commissioned in 1910. After a period on two-seaters, he became a *Jasta* pilot in May 1917, and soon began to shine as a fighter ace.

On 29 September von Schleich accounted for his 25th victory, and after a rest as a *Jastaschule* commander, he was given command of *Jagdgruppe* 8 in 1918, which eventually became JG IV. He rose to high rank in World War 2, but eventually died in 1947 due to ill health whilst still a British PoW. Although known for his all-black aircraft, von Schleich's 'normal' camouflaged Albatros of 1917 carried the Bavarian lion emblem on a blue and white diamond circle painted directly onto its varnished fuselage.

Emil Thuy, from Westphalia, was wounded as a soldier prior to aviation service. Via two-seaters in 1915, Thuy eventually ended up with *Jasta* 21 in early 1917, having claimed one kill with FFA33 in September

1915. Flying on the French front, he had achieved another 13 victories by September 1917 before being sent to command *Jasta* 28. Now serving on the British front, Thuy added several more kills to his tally on Albatros Scouts before *Jasta* 28 re-equipped with Fokker biplanes. He survived the war with 35 victories, and the *Pour le Mérite*, only to die in a flying accident whilst training pilots for the new Luftwaffe in the USSR in 1930.

Fritz Höhn had achieved 21 victories by war's end, the first ten whilst flying with *Jasta* 21 from late 1917 until he was wounded attacking a balloon on 20 April 1918. Most of these were probably scored flying an Albatros D V, although he also flew Pfalz fighters. Höhn, who later saw action with *Jastas* 81, 60 and 41, became known as something of a 'balloon-buster', for at least ten of his victories were against these dangerous targets. He was eventually killed in action by a French pilot from Spa 67 whilst flying a Fokker biplane on 3 October 1918.

Mention has already been made of Heinrich Claudius Kroll, who served with *Jasta* 9 prior to joining *Jasta* 24s as commander. The other star of the latter unit was yet another senior NCO pilot, Freidrich Altemeier, who was over 30 years of age during his most dangerous period at the front. Hailing from a town near Hanover, he had worked in the mighty Krupps factory pre-war, then served with the infantry. After being wounded, Altemeier moved to flying, and following a period on two-seaters in 1916, he finally got onto fighters in early 1917.

Heinrich Seywald of *Jasta* 23b with his Albatros D V. The pilot's personal marking takes the form of a black stylised 'S' on a black and white band. The black-bordered white band wrapped around the fuselage was the *Jasta* marking, supplemented in this case by additional black decor to the rear of the fuselage. Wings and tailplane were probably covered in five-colour lozenge fabric. Seywald scored six victories in 1918, commanding the *Jasta* from June, although he was wounded three weeks later. However, he returned in July and saw out the war with his command (*G VanWyngarden collection*)

Heinrich Kroll flew Albatros D V D.2214/17 whilst with *Jasta* 24. The 'Yin-Yang' design is repeated both on the top of the fuselage and underneath. The fuselage itself is apparently varnished and the rudder clear doped (*P Grosz via G VanWyngarden*)

Heinrich Kroll flew with *Jasta* 9 prior to going to *Jasta* 24 as *Staffelführer*. A combat wound sustained on 14 August 1918 put him out of the war, but he had received the *Blue Max* by this time, and raised his score to 33

Bruno Loerzer commanded *Jasta* 26 and later JG III. By war's end he had achieved 44 victories. A personal friend of Hermann Göring, with whom he flew in 1916-17, he later gained high office in the Luftwaffe

Loezer's Albatros D V D.2299/17 is seen in late 1917, when he was leader of *Jasta* 26. The whole fuselage and tail was decorated with the black and white bands of *Jasta* 26, while his personal emblem was a six-pointed star. Wings are lozenge fabric, covered with light rib tapes, and the wheel covers are grey (*G VanWyngarden collection*)

Jasta 24s was then based directly opposite the British front, and by the end of the year Altemeier had scored nine victories in air combat – this tally included four SPADs, two Sopwith Triplanes and a Nieuport Scout. He claimed an additional four confirmed victories with Albatros D Vs in early 1918, one of which proved to be the unit's 50th victory (pilots from *Jasta* 24s claimed 88 victories in total, with the last being scored on 10 November). This kill came on 22 March 1918, Altemeier beating Kroll to the 'half-century' by 20 minutes! Wounded three times during the war, Altemeier's final score reached 21.

Jasta 26 was jointly unique with *Jasta* 11 in that two brothers commanded it. Both Manfred and Lothar von Richthofen had each commanded the latter unit, while Bruno and his brother Fritz Loerzer led *Jasta* 26.

Bruno Loerzer, who has already been mentioned in this volume, was one of *Jasta* 26's most successful pilots. After flying two-seaters, then serving with a Fokker *Eindecker* unit (where he scored two victories), he commanded *Jasta* 26 from its formation in January 1917 until he took command of JG III the following February. During this time Loerzer amassed another 21 victories, and by the end of the war his score stood at 44 kills. A close friend of Hermann Göring, he gained high rank in the Luftwaffe and finally died in 1960.

Brother Fritz had been a pre-war religious student, so was called the 'Flying Pastor' by the other pilots. He had first served with *Jasta* 6 (one kill), then with his brother's unit, which he finally commanded when Bruno went to JG III. Fritz remained with *Jasta* 26 until 12 June 1918 – the day he was shot down and taken prisoner by Capt R C Phillips of No

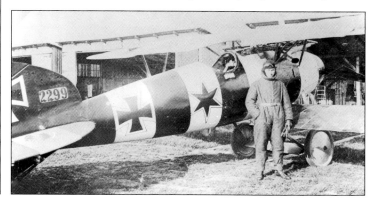

2 Sqn AFC. The German's score then stood at 11 victories. Fritz Loerzer died in 1952 when only 59

Otto Fruhner became the top scorer of *Jasta* 26 with 27 victories, and although he was nominated for the *Blue Max*, the Armistice came before its award. He had started his aviation service as a mechanic in late 1914, but soon found the desire to fly. Having served as a two-seater pilot on the Eastern Front, Fruhner then volunteered for single-seaters and ended up being posted to *Jasta* 26 – he had become an ace by early 1918. Like Bruno Loerzer, Fruhner also held high rank in the Luftwaffe. He died in June 1965.

Another successful Albatros pilot from *Jasta* 26 in 1917 was Xaver Dannhuber, whose first victory took the form of a balloon destroyed on 12 August. By 27 September he had became an ace, and during October he doubled his score, but was then injured whilst testing a Pfalz Scout with *Jasta* 79b, which he now commanded. Dannhuber did not make it back to the front until the final weeks of the war, although he did gain his 11th, and final, victory on 14 October 1918.

Walter Blume enjoyed a successful war flying with *Jasta* 9 in 1918, although he had actually cut his combat teeth with *Jasta* 26 in 1917. Born in Silesia, he was yet another future airman that suffered wounds in the early ground fighting with the army. Blume joined *Jasta* 26 via two-seater service in the spring of 1917, and by the end of that year had six victories to his credit. Then came the move to *Jasta* 9, with whom he won the *Pour le Mérite* on 2 October 1918, having scored most of his kills with the latter unit against the French. He died in 1964 aged 68 years.

After service with *Jasta* 26, Hermann Göring left to command *Jasta* 27 on 17 May 1917, having achieved seven victories thus far – two on two-seaters, one with a Fokker *Eindecker* and four with *Jasta* 26. Göring led numerous patrols and interceptions, and made

After serving with *Jasta* 26, Hermann Göring went on to command *Jasta* 27, and in this line-up of machines from the latter unit, seen at Iseghem airfield, his Albatros D V (D.1027/17?) can be seen nearest to the camera. There is a D III amongst them, and personal identification appears to be black numbers on a white fuselage band, while the leader's machine is devoid of white chevrons
(*P Grosz via G VanWyngarden*)

Hermann Göring, *Staffelführer* of *Jasta* 27. In all he scored (or at least claimed) 22 combat victories, the last as leader of JG I in 1918

several claims during 1917. By the end of that year he had been credited with 16 victories overall, and his combat report for 8 June 1917 (flying Albatros D III D.2049/17) tells us;

'Attack on a Nieuport which attacked me from above. I shot him down and followed him in a continuous spiral fight down. Repeatedly he turned upward, finally I forced him to land near Moorslede, where he somersaulted and burned the machine. The aerial fight was observed by the whole of *Jagdstaffel* 8 partly from the air and partially from the ground. According to my opinion as well as that of *Jasta* 8 there is no question of any other machine.'

This final comment seems to indicate that he was making sure no other pilot flying nearby would come along and take credit for the action. As it was, the British pilot involved, 2Lt F D Slee, from Perth, Western Australia, had been with his unit (No 1 Sqn, equipped with Nieuport Scouts) for just four days, and this was his first war flight. He was no match for the experienced Hermann Göring. Taken prisoner, Slee survived the war, and lived until 1967.

Later that summer Göring received an Albatros D V, and on 21 September he used the aircraft to down a Bristol Fighter crewed by both a pilot and observer that had achieved more aerial victories than he had. His report, whilst flying D V D.4424/17, states:

'Shortly after 9 am sighted an enemy *geschwader* of 14 aircraft (bombers), who were returning from Torhout in the direction of the front. I attacked with my escorts at an altitude of 4500 metres. I positioned myself close under the tail of an opponent and fired at him. I followed him closely with one of my other planes. Near Sleyhage, west of Roulers, the plane crashed. Pilot and observer were uninjured and the aircraft completely destroyed.'

Despite his comment, the pilot, Ralph Curtis, had been hit, and mortally wounded, which is why this experienced duo offered Göring so little opposition. He had obviously surprised them from their blind spot, and in air combat, one who doesn't watch every inch of the sky is always in danger of surprise attack. That in no way detracts from Göring's achievement. It was all part of the fighter pilot's trade to 'Destroy one's enemy, with minimum risk to yourself'.

Early in the New Year the unit received Triplanes, and Göring used the Dr I to increase his score to 21 by June – he had won the *Blue Max* after his 18th victory. He was given command of the prestigious JG I in mid-1918, and he gained his final kill in July.

It has to be said that a number of Göring's claims are highly suspect, with little evidence of a corresponding loss in British records. As most of the air fighting took place over the German side of the lines, wrecked Allied aircraft could usually be located in order to verify a German pilot's claim. However, it is interesting to note just how many were claimed after being seen to 'fall', or at least appear to go down, inside Allied lines. Frontline observers were usually asked to verify such scenes, and it is clear that what they may have seen did not always tie up with real events. This happened with a number of pilots, not just Göring, but one is left to wonder who was 'supporting' him at HQ. This question is easily posed because of his infamous future, but the facts remain nevertheless. He obviously had friends, and a 'presence'.

Willi Kampe was one of Göring's successful Albatros pilots. Another older senior NCO, he too had been a pre-war soldier, but after transferring to aviation, moved through two-seaters to fighters. Joining *Jasta* 27 in February 1917, Kampe was a slow starter, but between August and December he scored six victories, and in the early weeks of 1918 (flying Triplanes) he got two more. He was killed in action fighting Airco DH 4 bombers of No 27 Sqn on 8 March, scoring his last victory in this final engagement.

Helmut Dilthey was another 1917 scorer. He had joined the aviation service in late 1914, and then served on the Russian Front in two-seaters. He was assigned to *Jasta* 27 in May 1917, and gained five or six victories on the Albatros before being given command of *Jasta* 40s in April 1918. Dilthey scored one more kill before losing his life attacking an Airco DH 9 of No 107 Sqn, his aircraft appearing to have been hit by German flak.

Royal Württemberg *Jagdstaffel* 28's leading light was Max Müller. He too was older than the norm, being 27 at the outbreak of hostilities, and pre-war he had been an army mechanic and chauffeur. Müller transferred to the air service in 1913, and although he had become a pilot prior to the start of the war, he had subsequently broken both his legs in a serious crash, and this delayed his move to the frontline for some months.

When Müller finally got to fly two-seaters, he duly received several high decorations before transferring to fighters. After scoring five kills with *Jasta* 2, he moved to *Jasta* 28, with whom he increased his score to 29, before returning to *Jasta* 2. Müller was killed in action on 9 January 1918.

There are several photographs in existence of Müller's Albatros D V D.1154/17, which had a varnished fuselage, grey cowling and wheel covers and a yellow tailplane, with a single black stripe round each side. The upper wings were standard Mauve and green, with pale blue undersides,

Jasta 28w's leader Otto Hartmann (centre of photograph, with hands behind his back) and his pilots in 1917. At the rear, from left to right, are Ltn Lamprecht, Erwin Wenig (4 kills), Erich Weiss (2 kills) and Kurt Wittekund (2 kills). In the middle row, again from left to right, are Vfw Bärenfänger, Vfw Wagner, Ltn Koch, Hartmann, Karl Bolle (36 kills), Ernst Hess (17 kills) and Oblt Weber. Finally, in the front row from left to right, are Max Müller (36 kills), Franz Ray (17 kills) and August Hanko (5 kills)
(*G VanWyngarden collection*)

whilst the latter also had two large 'M' letters on the lower wing to help ground observers confirm his kills. The spinner was red and Müller's personal marking was a black comet-like image on the fuselage, edged in white, although the 'star' was circular and the two 'tails' resembled a sweeping 'V' on its side.

Another ace with *Jasta* 28 was Franz Ray, who downed eight British aircraft in 1917 following service with *Jasta* 1 in 1916. He eventually took command of *Jasta* 49 and ended the war with a total of 17 kills, all bar two of which were against the British.

The leader of *Jasta* 29, following in the footsteps of men like Erwin Böhme, Kurt Wolff and Otto Schmidt, was Harold Auffahrt. He had been an observer prior to pilot training, and had then seen action with *Jasta* 18 in the summer of 1917, becoming an ace during September. Once in command of *Jasta* 29, his score increased to 29 or maybe even 31 by war's end. Auffahrt would have added several kills to his *Jasta* 18 score while flying an Albatros, prior to moving on to the Fokker D VII in the early summer of 1918. He was proposed for the *Blue Max*, but the Armistice had come into effect before the award was approved. After the war he ran a flying school, and died in 1946.

Fritz Kieckhäfer was a 1917 Albatros ace with *Jasta* 29. Berlin-born, he scored one victory with *Jasta* 32 prior to be posted to *Jasta* 29. By the end of the year Kieckhäfer had scored a total of seven kills before a wound put him in hospital. Eventually returning to duty, he had added one more victory to his tally when he was wounded yet again, and this time he succumbed to his injuries on 7 June 1918.

Prussian *Jasta* 30 spent its whole war on the German 6th Army front. Hans Bethge came from *Jasta* 1 to command it, having already scored three kills with this unit. Another Berliner, Bethge who was 26, had spent the early war years flying two-seaters and then Fokker *Eindeckers*. During the course of 1917 he steadily added to his tally, which had reached 18 victories by the end of October, and in early 1918 he added two more. Nominated for the *Pour le Mérite*, Bethge's death in action on 17 March 1918, whilst flying a Pfalz D III, halted the process.

A native of Silesia, Hans-Georg von der Marwitz was the son of a general. A former Uhlan and then an infantryman, he transferred to the air service in 1916 and went onto two-seaters (one victory), prior to flying fighters. Whilst with *Jasta* 30 von der Marwitz scored at least five victories on the Albatros, but also flew the Pfalz D IIIa – by the end of October 1918 he had a total of 15 claims, and had occasionally commanded the unit. Having survived the war, von der Marwitz was killed in an aeroplane accident in May 1925.

Fellow *Jasta* 30 pilot Ltn Joachim von Bertrab shot down four British aeroplanes in two sorties during the morning of 6 April 1917 – the day America declared war on Germany. This was quite a feat at the time, and he went on to add a fifth kill in May, but on 12 August he was forced to crash-land in Allied territory after being wounded in an engagement with British ace, Lt Edward 'Mick' Mannock, of No 40 Sqn, who was flying a Nieuport Scout. Von Bertrab flew a distinctive black Albatros D III with white crosses and a comet insignia on the fuselage for much of his career as a fighter pilot, although by the time he was shot down he had progressed to an all-black D V.

Joachim von Bertrab of *Jasta* 30 scored five victories in the spring of 1917 – no fewer than four on 6 April. He was shot down, wounded, and taken prisoner on 12 August by Mick Mannock of No 40 Sqn

Many attempts have been made to describe Joachim von Bertrab's all-black Albatros seen in this photo. It now seems possible that the comet insignia was red with very light yellow edging. The national crosses were white on the fuselage (but edged in black) and all-white on the tail, but remained black, edged with white, on the upper wings, although these upper wing crosses were nearer the tips than normal. Wing undersurfaces were sky blue. While this author is not totally convinced the man standing by the machine is von Bertrab, it may well be. Upper wing areas were light green, dark green and reddish brown

Jasta 31 first saw action on the Western Front in early 1917, but in September the unit moved to Italy, where it operated until returning to France in early March 1918. It did not produce any Albatros, aces although several future aces with other *Jastas* opened their scores whilst part of the unit.

Jasta 32b likewise had a dearth of aces in 1917. Only Rudolf Windisch, from Dresden, made any sizeable score, claiming seven by January 1918 (plus an earlier kill while on two-seaters in 1916). A pre-war soldier, Windisch suffered an early wound in action which convinced him to move to aviation. When he finally became a fighter pilot, he scored his seven victories between September 1917 and January 1918, and was then moved briefly to *Jasta* 50, before being given command of *Jasta* 66 on 24 January. Windisch had raised his score to 22 by late May, with several of these probably being achieved in an Albatros, but he then failed to return from a patrol on the 27th of that same month. Believing the ace to be a

Jasta 31's Fritz Jacobsen (right) with Albatros D III D.2090/16 at Mars-sous-Bourcq on 6 April 1917. The black and white diamond band was his personal marking. Note the high windshield and an unusual fairing over the gun butts. The aircraft wears the normal camouflage patterns for the period (*D Gröschel via G VanWyngarden*)

Jacobsen's D.2090/16 is seen in the early summer of 1917. The entire upper fuselage has now been heavily mottled with rags or a sponge – the white spots may have been intended as flowers. Other *Jasta* 31 machines received similar mottling treatments (*D Gröschel via G VanWyngarden*)

prisoner, the German high command allowed his *Blue Max* nomination to be processed, and this was awarded in June. However, he did not come home at war's end, and the circumstances of his death still remain unclear, although it must be assumed that he died on, or around, the time of his loss date. It has to be wondered if he was killed by frontline French troops when he came down. The nearest suggestion is that he was 'killed while attempting to escape'. He was 21 years old.

The son of a police captain, Robert Greim, later Ritter von Greim, was a Bavarian from Bayreuth. Entering the army as a cadet in 1906, aged 14, he was commissioned into the Bavarian artillery in 1913, and saw action with this arm in the early months of the war. In August 1915 he moved into aviation, firstly as an observer, then a pilot. Von Greim had scored one victory on two-seaters by the time he joined *Jasta* 34b in April 1917, and just over a month later he began a scoring run that would last into the summer.

Robert Greim flew this Albatros D V whilst with *Jasta* 34b. Its whitish-silver fuselage was the unit identification marking, while Greim himself had two wide red bands painted around the fuselage and a red spinner as his personal markings. Finally, the aircraft's wings and tailplane were camouflaged in green and mauve. By the end of the war Greim had achieved 28 victories and been awarded the *Pour le Mérite*. He commanded *Jagdgruppen* 10 and 9 for periods in 1918 while still commanding *Jasta* 34 (*G VanWyngarden collection*)

One of the machines von Greim used during this time was D III D.643/17, which carried dark (red?) discs on the top and sides of the fuselage. With eight victories to his credit by early 1918, he was given command of *Jagdgruppe* Nr 10 – which included *Jasta* 34b – until July, at which time he was sent to lead JGr 9. He returned to command *Jasta* 34b in the closing weeks of the war, and survived the conflict with a tally of 28 victories, which had been scored flying Albatros D Vs, Triplanes and Fokker D VIIs. Awarded the *Blue Max* in October 1918, von Greim later became a Luftwaffe general in World War 2, and committed suicide in May 1945 following Germany's second defeat of the century.

Westphalian Heinrich Bongartz was the star-turn with *Jasta* 36, the former schoolteacher having served with the infantry against the French at Verdun. Commissioned whilst still in the field, he eventually decided to join the air service and went through the usual process before arriving on *Jasta* 36 in time to start scoring in April 1917. By the end of the year Bongartz had achieved 27 kills, including five kite balloons. He had become *Staffelführer* in September, but during his time with the unit was wounded on five separate occasions – the last injury, on 29 April 1918, put him out of the war. Bongartz had by this time claimed 33 kills, mostly on Albatros scouts, and won the *Pour le Mérite*. He died after World War 2.

Another successful ace with *Jasta* 36 was its leader from May 1917, Walter von Bülow-Bothkamp, who was born in April 1894 in Holstein. A former law student who had travelled extensively pre-war, he had scored victories on two-seaters in the Middle East with FA300 before joining *Jasta* 18 in December 1916. Raising his tally to 13, von Bülow-Bothkamp then went to *Jasta* 36b and scored a further 15 kills, for which he was awarded the *Blue Max* in October 1917. He was then given command of *Jasta* 2, but was shot down and killed by Capt W M Fry MC of No 23 Sqn on 6 January 1918.

Theodor Quandt achieved 15 victories in World War 1 with *Jasta* 36. A pre-war infantry officer and then artillery man, he served on both the Eastern and Western Fronts prior to moving into aviation. Via two-seaters, he arrived on *Jasta* 36 on 1 April 1917, and by the end of the year had scored eight victories on the British front – probably all on

Walter von Bülow-Bothkamp scored 28 victories in World War 1. Serving initially with FA300 in the Middle East in 1916, he joined *Jasta* 18 in France the following year, and from 10 May took command of *Jasta* 36. Von Bülow-Bothkamp won the *Pour le Mérite* and took command of *Jasta* Boelcke in December, but before adding to his score he was shot down by Capt Willie Fry MC of No 23 Sqn on 6 January 1918

Albatros machines. Taking command of *Jasta* 53, he failed to score again prior to returning to lead his former unit in the summer of 1918.

Hans Hoyer was another *Jasta* 36 Albatros ace, the 27-year-old from Rostock serving in the artillery at the outbreak of war. He subsequently won the coveted Knight's Cross of the Military St Henry Order in November 1915, and five months later moved into aviation. Serving initially on two-seaters until he joined *Jasta* 36 in late July 1917, Hoyer had achieved eight kills, and three unconfirmed, by early November. Made acting CO when his *staffel* leader was on leave, he was shot down and killed flying a D V by Capt P F Fullard of No 1 Sqn on 15 November.

Albert Dossenbach achieved his first nine victories on two-seaters (shared with his observer, Hans Schilling) during 1916, which was quite a score for this period. Indeed, he became the first two-seater pilot to win the *Blue Max*. In early 1917 Dossenbach was given command of *Jasta* 36, and during 'Bloody April' he downed five French aircraft to become an Albatros ace as well. Wounded by bomb splinters during a raid on his airfield, he recovered to take command of *Jasta* 10 in June. However, after adding one further scalp to his tally, Dossenbach was shot down and killed on 3 July while attacking a DH 4 bomber of No 57 Sqn, the ace being seen to either fall or jump from his burning Albatros.

Carl Degelow flew briefly with *Jasta* 36 – five days, to be exact! After accidentally wounding a fellow officer whilst practise shooting at ground targets, he was sent away to *Jasta* 7, commanded by Josef Jacobs. Degelow would later gain fame with *Jasta* 40, which he eventually led. He recorded some interesting observations about being a fighter pilot during this period;

'The great Manfred von Richthofen made a clear distinction between "hunters" and "shooters". The former were very deliberate, and did not open fire until they knew they could hit their prey; the latter always fired too soon and thereby wasted much valuable ammunition that might be needed to save their lives. A frequent occurrence was that from a great distance behind me an enemy single-seat fighter's guns were popping away. Immediately I knew the pilot was a beginner – a "shooter" – and that made me anticipate the fight with a great deal more confidence.'

Concerning his first air combat, in September 1917, Degelow recalled;

'The enemy plane I was attacking (a Bristol F 2b) seemed to have been assigned to protect the squadron's rear. Again and again I peppered him with lively machine gun volleys. His only reaction was to wave his arm. That broke the thread of my patience. I dived steeply on him and again pressed both buttons of my guns, but suddenly the "tak-tak-tak" ceased and, with dismay, I saw the empty cartridge belt flutter down into my cockpit. My ammunition was used up!

'(Now) my opponent turned and our roles were reversed. I was the hare and he the hound. The fellow did not shoot badly and soon smashed my oil tank, resulting in my goggles being covered with a fine spray of oil. Like a madman I jerked the control stick and tried with quick turns to evade the Englishman's fire.

"Only after a bitter curving flight was I able to escape my enemy. I (then) looked round in time to see my opponent dealt with by the proven "Konone" (ace), Ltn Jacobs, who made quick work of destroying the two-seater.'

Jasta 37's star in 1917 was Ernst Udet, who joined after enjoying great success with *Jasta* 15, and he later took command of the former unit. One supposes that if Allied airmen were always seeing the Red Baron, it follows that the Germans were always seeing one of the big Allied aces in the air. Shortly before he left *Jasta* 15, Udet lost a pilot under his command, and he later wrote that he may have met the French ace Georges Guynemer in combat;

'On 26 May 1917 we fly cover. We are at about 2000 metres altitude and the sky is clear – the sun beats down on us. From time to time I turn around and nod at the others who fly behind me; the Wendel brothers, Puz and Glinkermann – everything as is it should be.

'I don't know if there is such a thing as a sixth sense, but suddenly I'm certain we are in some sort of danger. I make a half turn – and in that instant I see, close to my side, not 20 metres off, Puz's aircraft enveloped

Jasta 15's Ltn Ernst Udet stands in front of Albatros D III D.1941/16 on 1 January 1917 at Habsheim airfield. Mechanics Gunkelmann and Behrend can be seen working on the engine. The aircraft has a reddish-brown stained fuselage and camouflaged rudder
(*G VanWyngarden collection*)

Ernst Udet's black Albatros D Va, which he used with *Jasta* 37 in the winter of 1917-18. The *LO* personal insignia was an abbreviation of his fiancé's name, Eleonore Zink, whom he called 'Lo'
(*P Grosz via G VanWyngarden*)

Udet is seen wearing an RFC flying coat, much favoured by German pilots, standing next to his Albatros D Va. Most *Jasta* 37 aircraft carried a white number on the nose, and under the lower wing, whereas Udet had a white chevron and a large black 'U' under the port wing. Two white lines also appeared on the top wing just inboard of the crosses (*P Grosz via G VanWyngarden*)

Hans Waldhausen and groundcrew stand in front of his Albatros D V D.2284/17. This was the machine in which he was captured on 27 September 1917

in fire and smoke. But Puz himself sits straight up in the centre of this inferno, head turned towards me. He slowly lifts his right arm to his crash helmet. It could be the last convulsion, but it looks as though he were saluting me – for the last time.

'Then his machine breaks up. The fuselage dives straight down like a fiery meteor, the broken wing planes trundling after it. I am stunned as I stare over the side after the wreckage. An aircraft moves into the range of my sight and tears westward about 500 metres below me. At the same moment I have the feeling that it can only be Guynemer!

'I push down, I have to get him! But the wings of my Albatros are not up to the strain. They begin to flutter more and more, so that I fear the machine will disintegrate in the air. I give up the chase and return home.'

Postwar research has revealed that it was not Guynemer who shot down Ltn Eberhard 'Puz' Hänisch.

Udet brought his score to 20 with *Jasta* 37, and was then recruited by Baron von Richthofen to command his *Jasta* 11 in the spring of 1918, followed in turn by *Jasta* 4. Whilst with *Jasta* 37, both Udet and Hans Waldhausen had been the unit's main scorers. The latter individual, like any number of World War 1 fighter aces, achieved brief glory and then faded from the scene.

A pre-war army cadet, Waldhausen saw action with the artillery in the early days of the conflict. After being wounded, he transferred to aviation, firstly as an observer, then a pilot. In July 1917 he arrived at *Jasta* 37, and for some unexplained reason he soon became known as 'The Eagle of Lens'. During just nine days in the latter half of September, he achieved

six victories, plus another unconfirmed, although none of these kills related directly to Lens. Waldhausen scored single victories on the 19th, 24th and 25th, and downed two balloons and an RE 8 on the 27th, again some way south of Lens. However, on this last evening he was attacked and shot down by two experienced fighter pilots, one of whom was with the RFC and the other with the RNAS. The former was Lt J H Tudhope of No 40 Sqn, and the latter Flt Cdr C D Booker of 8 Naval Squadron. Tudhope's combat report recorded;

'At 6.50 pm I was sitting in my machine on the Advanced Landing Ground when I observed an Albatros Scout under AA fire approaching one of our balloons.

'I immediately started the engine and took off, heading straight for the E.A., and when about 1000 ft up observed E.A. firing into the balloon. E.A. passed over and west of balloon before turning, by which time I was directly between E.A and the lines.

'I then attacked and fired a burst of about 30 rounds at very close range into E.A., who dived and manoeuvred but was unable to put any distance between himself and Nieuport.

'I fired two more bursts, almost crashing into E.A. on the second. E.A. immediately turned West and went down very steeply with engine stopped and Nieuport above. E.A. went straight down and crashed alongside the light railway station at Souchez. Nieuport came right down and circled round E.A. which was immediately surrounded by troops.

'During engagement a second Nieuport approached from the East and fired a few rounds at long range. Shots were also observed being fired apparently from the ground.'

In fact the other aeroplane was a Sopwith Camel, not a Nieuport.

Taken prisoner, Waldhausen remained incarcerated until the end of the war, after which he studied law and rose to the position of judge in Germany. He later served with the Luftwaffe during World War 2, and died in November 1976.

Otto Rosenfeld scored his first four victories with *Jasta* 12 in May and June 1917. He had come to fighters via two-seaters, but a wound on 12 June put him in hospital. Once back in action, he moved to *Jasta* 41, and by the end of the year had increased his score to eight. However, by this date Rosenfeld was a prisoner, having been brought down during a balloon attack on 29 December. He managed to escape and return to his unit in April 1918, although in retrospect he would have been better to have remained in captivity. Although he added a further five victories in the early summer, he eventually fell in combat on 7 July, probably after a fight with the Nieuport 28s of the American 95th Aero Squadron.

Helmut Dilthey, leader of *Jasta* 40s, sits in his D Va painted in Saxon colours of green and white. Note the tubular sight protruding through the windshield, the rear-view mirror and the two ring-sights on each gun. Dilthey was probably flying this machine on 9 July 1918, the day he was hit by German AA fire during an attack on an RAF DH 9 bomber (*Rosenstein album via G Williams*)

Albatros D III (OAW) flown by Günther Dobberke in *Jasta* 45 (or perhaps *Jasta* 60) in the spring of 1918. His personal name abbreviation *DO*. is possibly finished in white, with black edging. The colours of the tail and wing bands are not confirmed, although the wings are of lozenge fabric. Dobberke claimed eight victories in World War 1, all but one with *Jasta* 60 from May
(*P Grosz via G VanWyngarden*)

Albert Dietlen scored five victories with *Jasta* 41 in early 1918, the 28-year-old Bavarian having earlier been an observer in two-seaters during 1916. He had gained one victory whilst serving with the *Abteilung* unit, then doubled his score with a second kill as a fighter pilot with *Jasta* 23b in August 1917. Dietlen then moved to *Jasta* 58 as leader, where he added two more victories in April before he was killed when his Albatros D V was shot down in a fight with Camels of No 43 Sqn.

Robert Heibert joined the army in August 1914, and on transferring to the air service in May 1915 came to fighters via two-seaters. During the war he was wounded four times. He gained his first kill with *Jasta* 33 in August 1917, then joined *Jasta* 46 upon its formation in December of that same year. In the spring of 1918 Heibert (*text continues on page 79*)

Konrad Brendel flew with *Jasta* 45 after serving with *Jasta* 17. He achieved nine victories before being shot down and killed by ground fire on 2 September 1918. This photograph shows him seated in his *Jasta* 17 Albatros D Va, which was marked with diagonal light coloured stripes on the varnished ply fuselage. A white fin and rudder comprised the unit marking. Note the flare signal cartridges and holder immediately below the cockpit (*HAC/UTD via G VanWyngarden*)

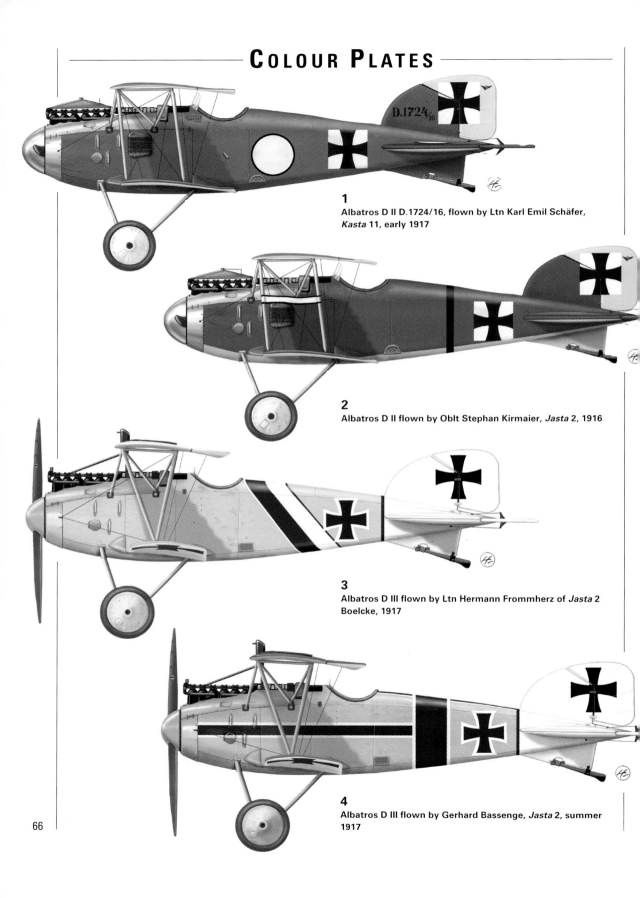

1
Albatros D II D.1724/16, flown by Ltn Karl Emil Schäfer,
Kasta 11, early 1917

2
Albatros D II flown by Oblt Stephan Kirmaier, *Jasta* 2, 1916

3
Albatros D III flown by Ltn Hermann Frommherz of *Jasta* 2
Boelcke, 1917

4
Albatros D III flown by Gerhard Bassenge, *Jasta* 2, summer
1917

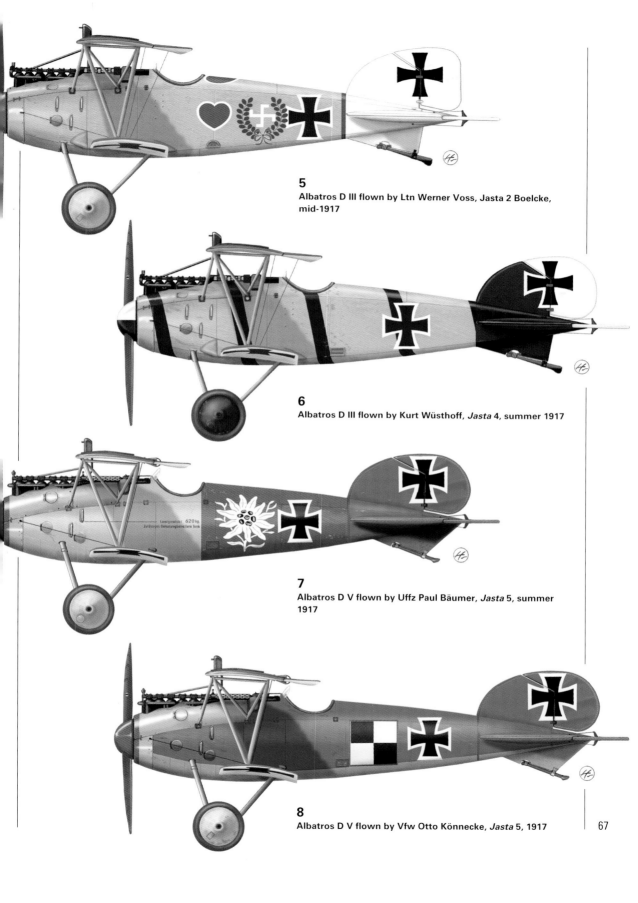

5
Albatros D III flown by Ltn Werner Voss, Jasta 2 Boelcke, mid-1917

6
Albatros D III flown by Kurt Wüsthoff, *Jasta* 4, summer 1917

7
Albatros D V flown by Uffz Paul Bäumer, *Jasta* 5, summer 1917

8
Albatros D V flown by Vfw Otto Könnecke, *Jasta* 5, 1917

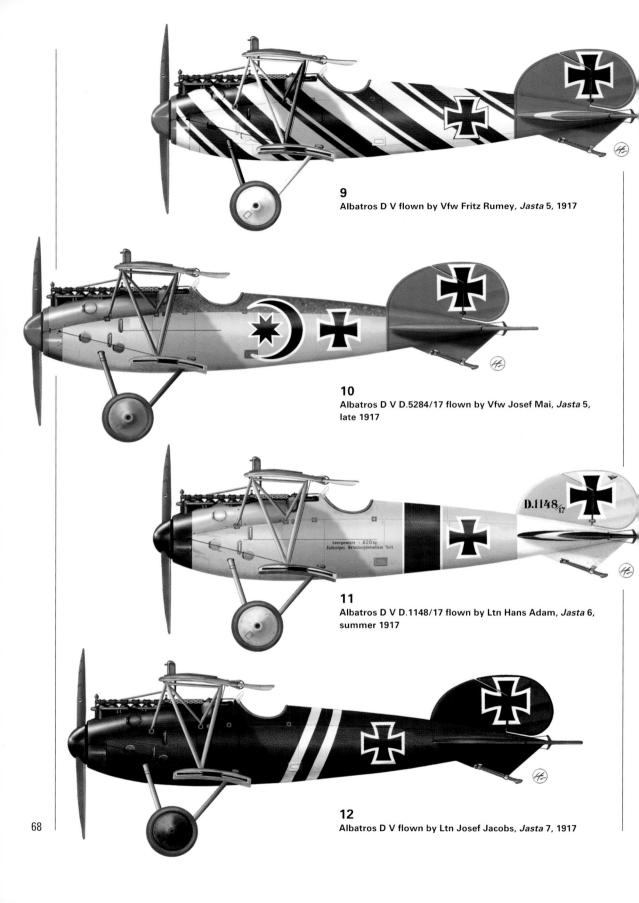

9
Albatros D V flown by Vfw Fritz Rumey, *Jasta* 5, 1917

10
Albatros D V D.5284/17 flown by Vfw Josef Mai, *Jasta* 5, late 1917

11
Albatros D V D.1148/17 flown by Ltn Hans Adam, *Jasta* 6, summer 1917

12
Albatros D V flown by Ltn Josef Jacobs, *Jasta* 7, 1917

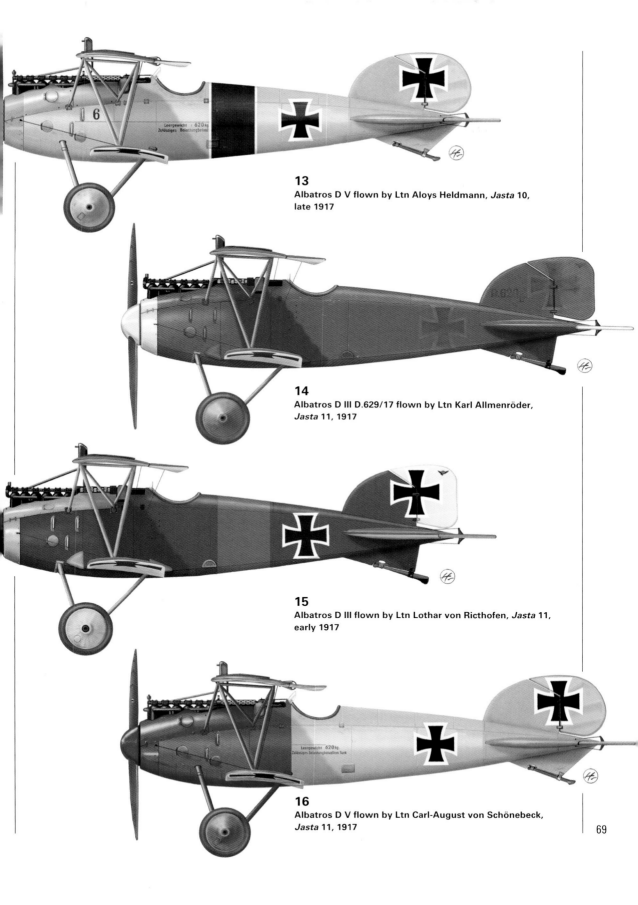

13
Albatros D V flown by Ltn Aloys Heldmann, *Jasta* 10,
late 1917

14
Albatros D III D.629/17 flown by Ltn Karl Allmenröder,
Jasta 11, 1917

15
Albatros D III flown by Ltn Lothar von Ricthofen, *Jasta* 11,
early 1917

16
Albatros D V flown by Ltn Carl-August von Schönebeck,
Jasta 11, 1917

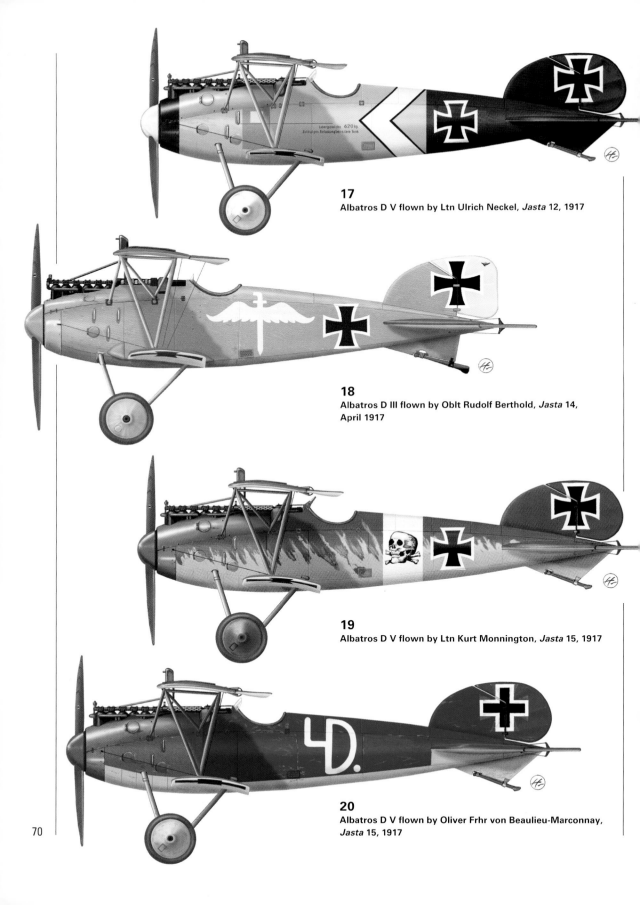

17
Albatros D V flown by Ltn Ulrich Neckel, *Jasta* 12, 1917

18
Albatros D III flown by Oblt Rudolf Berthold, *Jasta* 14,
April 1917

19
Albatros D V flown by Ltn Kurt Monnington, *Jasta* 15, 1917

20
Albatros D V flown by Oliver Frhr von Beaulieu-Marconnay,
Jasta 15, 1917

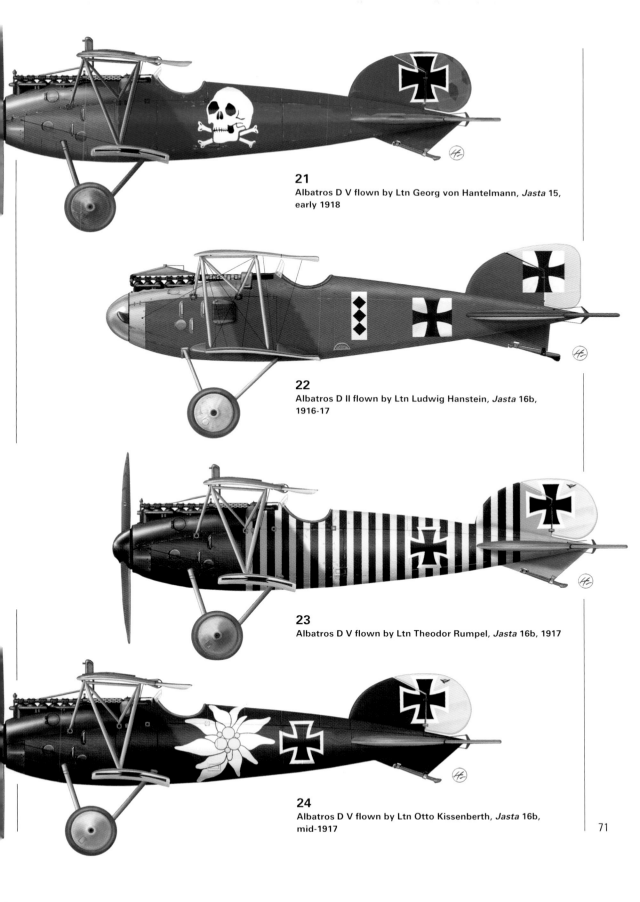

21
Albatros D V flown by Ltn Georg von Hantelmann, *Jasta* 15,
early 1918

22
Albatros D II flown by Ltn Ludwig Hanstein, *Jasta* 16b,
1916-17

23
Albatros D V flown by Ltn Theodor Rumpel, *Jasta* 16b, 1917

24
Albatros D V flown by Ltn Otto Kissenberth, *Jasta* 16b,
mid-1917

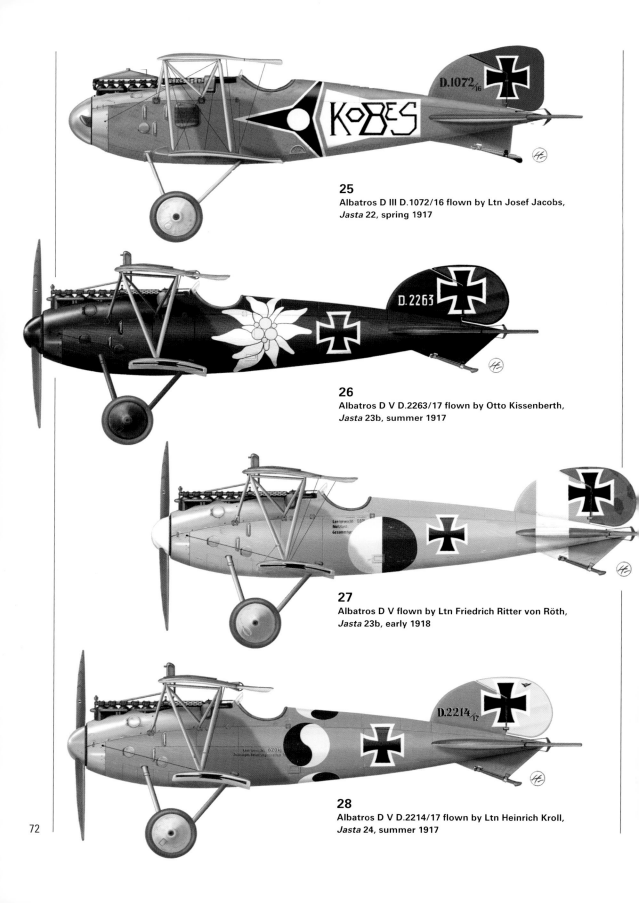

25
Albatros D III D.1072/16 flown by Ltn Josef Jacobs,
Jasta 22, spring 1917

26
Albatros D V D.2263/17 flown by Otto Kissenberth,
Jasta 23b, summer 1917

27
Albatros D V flown by Ltn Friedrich Ritter von Röth,
Jasta 23b, early 1918

28
Albatros D V D.2214/17 flown by Ltn Heinrich Kroll,
Jasta 24, summer 1917

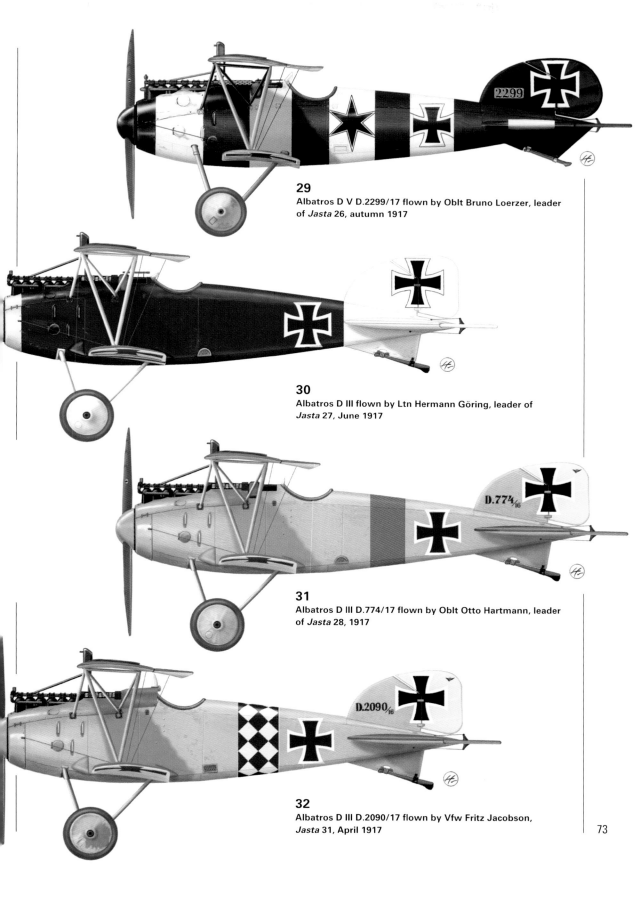

29
Albatros D V D.2299/17 flown by Oblt Bruno Loerzer, leader of *Jasta* 26, autumn 1917

30
Albatros D III flown by Ltn Hermann Göring, leader of *Jasta* 27, June 1917

31
Albatros D III D.774/17 flown by Oblt Otto Hartmann, leader of *Jasta* 28, 1917

32
Albatros D III D.2090/17 flown by Vfw Fritz Jacobson, *Jasta* 31, April 1917

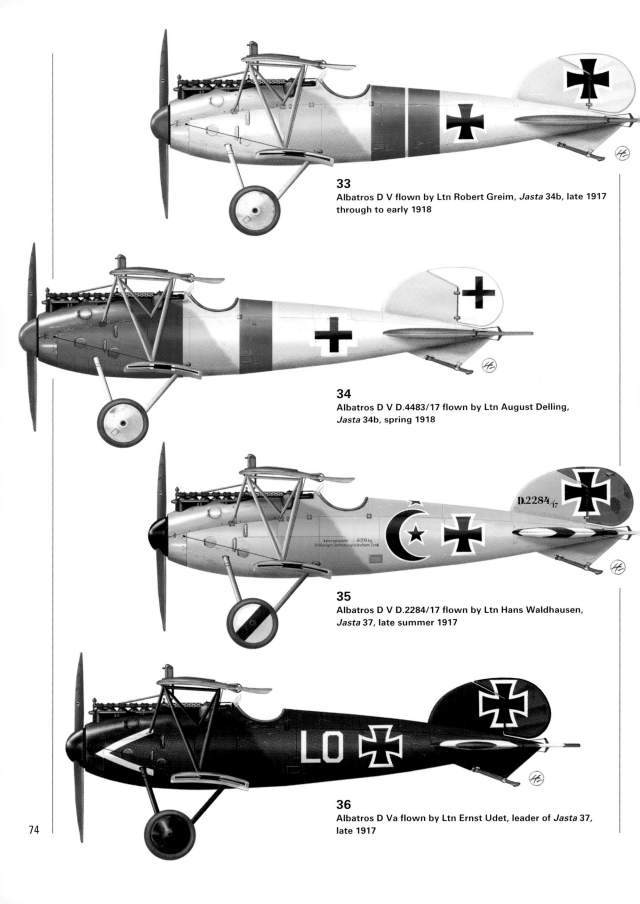

33
Albatros D V flown by Ltn Robert Greim, *Jasta* 34b, late 1917 through to early 1918

34
Albatros D V D.4483/17 flown by Ltn August Delling, *Jasta* 34b, spring 1918

35
Albatros D V D.2284/17 flown by Ltn Hans Waldhausen, *Jasta* 37, late summer 1917

36
Albatros D Va flown by Ltn Ernst Udet, leader of *Jasta* 37, late 1917

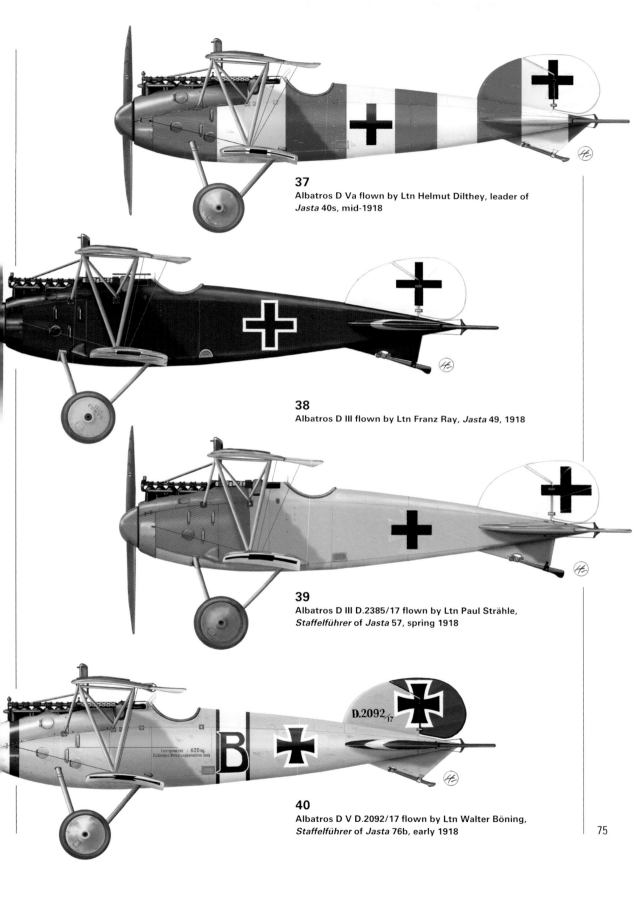

37
Albatros D Va flown by Ltn Helmut Dilthey, leader of
Jasta 40s, mid-1918

38
Albatros D III flown by Ltn Franz Ray, *Jasta* 49, 1918

39
Albatros D III D.2385/17 flown by Ltn Paul Strähle,
Staffelführer of *Jasta* 57, spring 1918

40
Albatros D V D.2092/17 flown by Ltn Walter Böning,
Staffelführer of *Jasta* 76b, early 1918

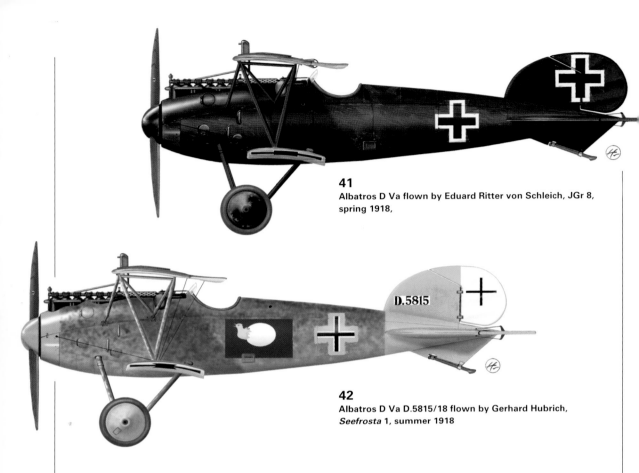

41
Albatros D Va flown by Eduard Ritter von Schleich, JGr 8,
spring 1918,

42
Albatros D Va D.5815/18 flown by Gerhard Hubrich,
Seefrosta 1, summer 1918

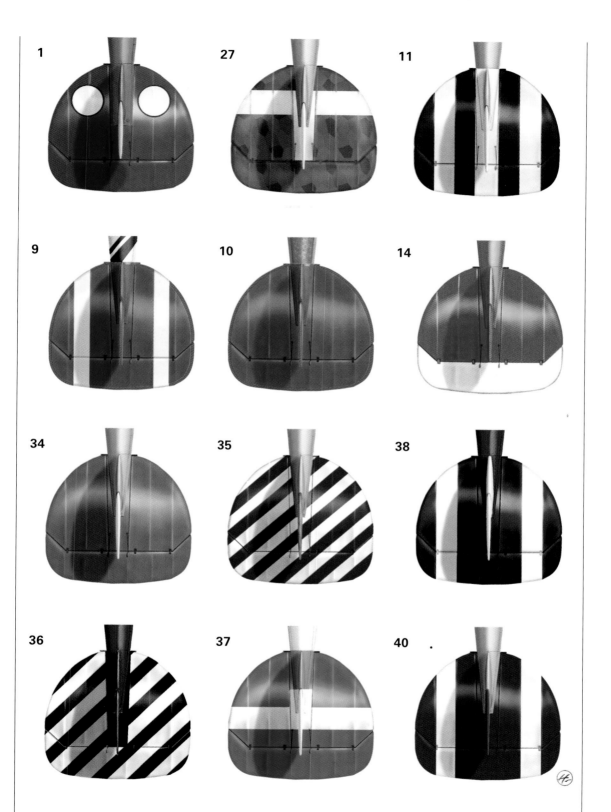

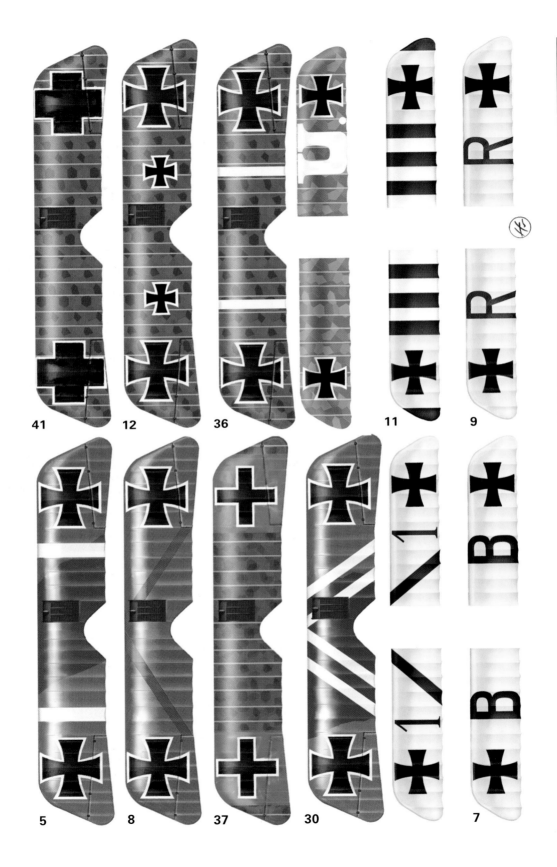

41

12

36

11

9

5

8

37

30

7

brought his score to five, the unit flying a mixture of Albatros D Vs and Pfalz D IIIs during this time – it is believed that he scored many of his victories on the former type. Heibert ended his scoring run on Fokker D VIIs in August, by which time he had claimed 13 kills. He subsequently took his own life in May 1933.

When Ltn Paul Strähle took command of *Jasta* 57 in January 1918 he was already an Albatros ace, having scored seven kills with *Jasta* 18 in 1917. Born in Würrtemburg in May 1893, and following the usual two-seat period, he joined the fighter unit in October 1916. Whilst with *Jasta* 57 he flew an Albatros D III and a D V, and he used these to add at least two further victories to his total before the arrival of the Fokker D VII.

Jasta 62 was one unit which flew Albatros D Vs well into 1918, and its star was Max Näther, whose personal Albatros boasted a 'fluttering' black, white and red flag on a flagpole, on a white rectangle, painted on its fuse-

Franz Schleiff, Staffelführer of *Jasta* 56 in 1918, poses with his Albatros D Va. Previously with FA300 in the Middle East, and then *Jasta* 41 in France. He gained twelve official victories, with nine more unconfirmed, before a serious wound on 27 March 1918 resulted in the amputation of his left hand. This D Va appears to be entirely overpainted, possibly in light blue-grey, with yellow trim – these were later the colours of *Jasta* 56. Note that the white edges of the crosses have been increased from the norm, and that the aircraft lacks a fuselage cross (*P Grosz via G VanWyngarden*)

Albatros D III (OAW) of *Jasta* 57 in flight in the spring of 1918. This aircraft is possibly Paul Strähle's machine D.2385/17, which he flew for three months from 24 February 1918, alternating with his D V D.4594/17. *Staffel* marking was a pale blue fuselage, with personal markings of different coloured noses to the end of the top cowling panel. The nose of D.2385 was red, as were the wheel covers. Wings and tailplane were in lozenge fabric, whilst the fin and rudder were white. Strähle downed his eighth and ninth victories in this machine on 17 April 1918 (*Hitschler/P Grosz via G VanWyngarden*)

Ltn Paul Strähle served with both *Jastas* 18 and 57 in 1917-18, scoring 15 victories. He survived the war

Martin Johns scored seven victories with *Jasta* 63 in 1918, making him the unit's top scorer. His OAW-built Albatros D Va carried a black 'J' on the fuselage just aft of the cockpit. The flare tube can just be seen to the left of Johns' head, as well as the unusual fairing over the guns. The white square beneath the weights table was a clear celluloid envelope for rigging diagrams. At this time *Jasta* 63's unit marking consisted of a large black diamond shape painted on the yellow clear-varnished plywood, resulting in a pattern of black and 'yellow' diamonds (*HAC/UTD via G VanWyngarden*)

lage sides. At aged 18 he was the youngest of the German aces, having been born in August 1899. Despite this, Näther had already seen action with the infantry, and been wounded. Assigned to *Jasta* 62 in March 1918, he gained eight victories and then, despite his tender years, was made *Staffelführer*. Later, flying D VIIs, Näther would bring his total to 26, which represented more than half of *Jasta* 62's final wartime tally of 48 kills. Although deservedly nominated for the *Blue Max*, he was denied his award by the Armistice.

Two months later Näther was involved in the German border war with Poland, during which he was shot down and killed on 8 January 1919. He was still only 19.

FINAL DAYS OF THE ALBATROS SCOUT

The *Jastas* that formed between December 1917 and early 1918 were generally equipped with Albatros D Vs and Pfalz D IIIs. These types had become the workhorses of the fighter units, who also periodically used the Fokker Triplane, which had first entered service with JG I in September

Hasso von Wedel of *Jasta* 75 used this Albatros D Va in the summer of 1918. His personal marking was a red 'richtrad' – a medieval execution wheel. A white fin and rudder was the unit marking, together with the black band, edged in white, by the tail. The spinner and metal panels were painted grey, as were the wheel covers. The aircraft had a natural varnish fuselage and wings covered in lozenge fabric, while the tailplane was striped both chordwise and spanwise on top and underneath. A close inspection of the photograph shows that the rudder cross was of the earlier, shorter length, and has been overpainted. The area around the fuselage cross has also been overpainted in order to show the Balkenkreuz over the Iron Cross (*P Grosz via G VanWyngarden*)

1917. Von Richthofen and his pilots generally liked the Fokker fighter, but a number of in-flight failures with the aircraft's top wing in late October cast a doubt over the machine's structural integrity until December, when this problem was rectified.

Jastas continued to employ a mix of fighters (even older D IIIs) well into the last year of the war. The size of these new units was somewhat smaller than the earlier *Jastas* due to pilot availability and machine production. Little size comparison can be made with Allied fighter units of the time, but as the British generally operated in just flight size (all three flights were sent aloft only on special occasions), it could be said that the opponents were evenly matched on a one-to-one basis.

The new Fokker biplane fighter was promised for the late spring or early summer of 1918, but until then the *Jastas* struggled on with what they had. From an ace's point of view, many of the subsequently successful Fokker biplane pilots gained combat experience on either the Albatros, Pfalz or Fokker Triplane during the spring of 1918, while established aces still flew them successfully in air actions on both the French and British fronts. However, due to this mix of machines it is difficult to be certain of who was flying what during this period.

Hasso von Wedel commanded *Jasta* 75 and later *Jasta* 24 after initial service with *Jasta* 14. He scored five victories in World War 1 and was later shot down over England flying a Me 109E with JG 3 during the Battle of Britain in 1940. Taken prisoner, von Wedel was repatriated towards the end of the war, and died defending Berlin in the last days of World War 2, aged 51

— Home Defence —

Albatros and Pfalz fighters also went to the Home Defence units known as the *Kampfeinsitzer Staffels*, or *Kests*. In the main, these small units were formed to defend the indus-

Walter Böning of *Jastas* 19 and 76b
stands by his Albatros D V
D.2092/17. It carries a black *B* on a
black and white fuselage band as his
personal insignia. Böning apparently
flew this D V with *Jasta* 19 at St
Loup in August 1917, and may have
taken it with him when he was
transferred to *Jasta* 76b. A severe
wound during a fight with Camels of
No 70 Sqn on 30 May 1918, in D Va
D.5765/17, put him out of the war
after claiming 17 victories
(*HAC/UTD via G VanWyngarden*)

trial targets in western Germany, which were mostly attacked by French
and British bombers – especially in 1918 by DH 4 and DH 9 aircraft of
the Independent Air Force (IAF). A variety of aces or future aces passed
through some of these *Kests*, the experienced ones either on a brief rest, or
merely assigned to give the other pilots the benefit of their experience.

There were no *Kest* aces produced, but several pilots scored victories as
the summer progressed, and the depredations of the IAF continued. The
persistence of the latter force eventually saw the *Kests* equipped with
Fokker D VIIs, and these were regularly operated in mixed flights with
Albatros D Vs and rotary-engined types like the Fokker D VI or Pfalz D
VIII.

MARINE FELD JASTAS

Areas of fighter operations by the *Marine Feld Jastas* (MFJs) were generally confined to the North Sea coast and just inland over Belgium. They
too had a variety of aircraft, flying not only Albatros D IIIs and D Vs, but
also Pfalz D IIIs. In the main, their opponents were the bombers and
fighters of the RNAS, and between them they fought a seemingly private
war up along the North Sea coast. RNAS aviators were constantly target-
ing places such as Ostende and Zeebrugge, as well as shipping and U-
boats from their bases around Dunkirk. Even after the RFC and RNAS
had merged to form the RAF on 1 April 1918, the ex-naval squadrons
continued to fight their 'private' war.

MFJ I was in action in the spring of 1917, and one of its leading pilots was Gotthard Sachsenberg. A former naval cadet, he became an observer with a Marine two-seater unit before taking pilot training. He then flew Fokker *Eindeckers* until assuming command of MFJ I in February 1917. By the end of the year Sachsenberg had scored eight victories, and he continued to lead the unit well into the summer of 1918, by which time the Fokker D VII had arrived. He won the *Pour le Mérite* in September 1918, and ended the war as commander of the Marine's only *Jagdgeschwader*, MJGr I. Sachsenberg's final tally stood at 31 kills, with many of his early successes having been claimed whilst flying the Albatros. He died in 1961.

Bertram Heinrich was one of Sachsenberg's pilots, flying both Albatros D IIIs and D Vs. Having shot down nine British aeroplanes in 1917, he in turn fell victim to Canadian pilot, Flt Cdr A M Shook, from the Camel-equipped 4 Naval Squadron on 22 March 1918. Wounded in the crash of his Albatros D V, Heinrich eventually returned to fly D VIIs with the unit in the summer, raising his score to 12. He then fell victim to a Camel yet again, future RAF ace Lt W S Jenkins of No 210 Sqn sending the German to his death on 31 August.

Theodor ('Theo') Osterkamp was another of MFJ I's successful pilots in early 1917. This 25-year-old Rhinelander achieved six victories during 1917, downing RFC and French scouts, plus at least one Belgian machine. He then went to command MFJ II in October, and by the early summer of 1918 Osterkamp had more than doubled

This Albatros D Va was flown by Walter Böning during his time with *Jasta* 76b. The tailplane shows the unit's blue and white marking, while the rear fuselage is painted in the blue and white diamond pattern of the Bavarian *Wappenschild* coat-of-arms. The machine was photographed whilst up on a trestle having its guns test-fired into the distant butts
(*Krüger/Grosz via G VanWyngarden*)

Hans Böhning of *Jasta* 79b had previously flown with *Jastas* 36 and 76. His early victories were scored on the Albatros Scout, and he ended the war with 17 victories. One of his D Vs had blue and white stripes round its fuselage

Eduard Ritter von Schleich is seen during his time as leader of *Jagdgruppe* 8, his black Albatros D Va having previously been used by Otto Kissenberth. Von Schleich was known as the 'Black Knight', and the D V he used with *Jasta* 32b was totally black, with just a white spinner (*G VanWyngarden collection*)

Gotthard Sachsenberg was a Marine ace with MFJ I, and he went on to command MFJGr I. He ended the war with 31 victories, and the *Pour le Mérite.* This Albatros D III does not have any specific markings, although it seems to have the usual grey spinner and panelling, and a clear-doped rudder. Note the substantial step-ladder (*G VanWyngarden collection*)

his score. A *Blue Max* winner, he survived the war with 32 victories, to which he later added a further six in 1940 as commander of World War 2 fighter unit JG 51. 'Uncle Theo' Osterkamp later rose to high rank in the Luftwaffe, and eventually died in January 1975.

Forerunner to the five MFJ units was the *Seefrontstaffel* (SFS), which flew a mixture of Albatros and Pfalz Scouts. Christian Kairies, Reinhold Poss and Gerhard Hubrich were three successful pilots who may have achieved five victories on the Albatros prior to postings to MFJ V, IV, and IV respectively, where they made further claims. Hubrich and Poss survived the war with 12 and 11 kills each, whilst Kairies died of wounds inflicted during combat with Camels of No 210 Sqn on 2 October 1918.

Gerhard Hubrich's Albatros D Va D.5815/17 of *Marine Feld Jasta* IV in late 1918. Its nose and tail were painted chrome yellow. Hubrich ended the war with 12 victories, having seen prior service with the *Seefrontstaffel* (*G VanWyngarden collection*)

SUMMATION

By the end of the war the Albatros Scouts had become the workhorse of the German Air Service. Although other fighters such as the Fokker Dr I Triplane or D VII more readily come to mind, the Albatros was the only type to see action throughout the 1916-18 period. And although purists might, quite rightly, feel that there was a vast difference between the D I and the D V, the name 'Albatros' nevertheless remains prominent in the flying history of World War 1. Indeed, aside from the extensive action it saw on the Western Front, Albatros Scouts also fought the Allies over Italy, in the Middle East and on the Eastern Front. All the major aces of the mid-war years had flown them, helping these highly skilled individuals carve out their own place in military aviation history.

All of these aces were *Blue Max* winners, and all them scored heavily with Albatros fighters. They are, from left to right, Karl Bolle (36 kills), Josef Veltjens (35 kills), Josef Jacobs (47 kills), Oskar von Boenigk (26 kills), Eduard von Schleich (35 kills), Ernst Udet (62 kills), Bruno Loerzer (44 kills) Paul Bäumer (43 kills), Hermann Göring (22 kills) and Heinrich Bongartz (33 kills). Between them, they accounted for 383 Allied aircraft and balloons (*F W Bailey*)

APPENDICES

Jadgstaffeln and their allegiances

Prussian

1, 2, 3, 4, 5, 6, 7, 8, 9, 10, 11, 12, 13, 14, 15, 17, 18, 19, 20, 25, 26, 27, 29, 30, 31, 33, 36, 37, 38, 39, 41, 42, 43, 45, 46, 48, 49, 50, 51, 52, 53, 55, 56, 57, 58, 59, 60, 61, 62, 63, 65, 66, 67, 68, 69, 70, 71, 73, 74, 75, 81, 82, 83, 85, 86, 87 88, 89, 90

Bavarian

16, 23, 32, 34, 35, 76, 77, 78, 79, 80

Saxon

21, 22, 24, 40, 44, 54, 72

Württemberg

28, 47, 64, 84

German Aces awarded the *Pour le Mérite* while mainly Albatros Scout pilots

Oblt Rudolf Berthold	*Jasta* 14	12/10/16
Ltn Gustav Leffers	*Jasta* 1	5/11/16
Oblt Hans Berr	*Jasta* 5	4/12/16
Ltn Manfred Fr von Richthofen	*Jasta* 2	12/1/17
Ltn Werner Voss	*Jasta* 2	8/4/17
Ltn Fritz Otto Bernert	*Jasta* 2	23/4/17
Ltn Karl Emil Schäfer	*Jasta* 11	26/4/17
Ltn Kurt Wolff	*Jasta* 11	4/5/17
Ltn Lothar Fr von Richthofen	*Jasta* 11	14/5/17
Ltn Heinrich Gontermann	*Jasta* 15	14/5/17
Ltn Karl Allmenröder	*Jasta* 11	14/6/17
Oblt Adolf Ritter von Tutschek	*Jasta* 12	3/8/17
Oblt Eduard Ritter von Dostler	*Jasta* 6	6/8/17
Ltn Max Ritter von Müller	*Jasta* 28w	3/9/17
Ltn Walter von Bülow-Bothkamp	*Jasta* 36	8/10/17
Ltn Kurt Wüsthoff	*Jasta* 4	22/11/17
Ltn Erwin Böhme	*Jasta* 2	24/11/17
Ltn Julius Buckler	*Jasta* 17	4/12/17
Ltn Hans Klein	*Jasta* 10	4/12/17
Oblt Eduard Ritter von Schleich	*Jasta* 21s	4/12/17
Ltn Heinrich Bongartz	*Jasta* 36	23/12/17
Oblt Bruno Leorzer	*Jasta* 26	12/2/18
Ltn Heinrich Kroll	*Jasta* 24s	29/3/18
Ltn Ernst Udet	*Jasta* 37	9/4/18
Ltn Karl Menckhoff	*Jasta* 72s	23/4/18
Ltn Fritz Pütter	*Jasta* 68	31/5/18
Oblt Hermann Göring	*Jasta* 27	2/6/18
Ltn Rudolf Windisch	*Jasta* 66	6/6/18
Ltn Otto Kissenberth	*Jasta* 23b	30/6/18

Jasta 11's Victories during April 1917

Date	Pilot	Br type	Sqn	Location	G/B	Pilot's total
2nd	Oblt M von Richthofen	BE 2d	13	Farbus	GS	32
"	Ltn K Allmenröder	BE 2	13	Angres	Lines	5
"	Vfw S Festner	FE 2d	57	SE Auby	GS	3
"	Ltn C Krefft	FE 2d	57	Dignies	GS	2
"	Oblt M von Richthofen	Sopwith 2	43	Givenchy	GS	33
3rd	Oblt M von Richthofen	FE 2d	43	Cité St Pierre	GS	34
"	Ltn K Schäfer	FE 2d	25	La Coulette	GS	9
5th	Oblt M Von Richthofen	Bristol F 2a	48	Lewarde	GS	35
"	Vfw S Festner	Bristol F 2a	48	Aniche	GS	4
"	Ltn G Simon	Bristol F 2a	48	N Monchecourt	GS	1
"	Oblt M von Richthofen	Bristol F 2a	48	Quincy	GS	36
"	Vfw S Festner	Nieuport 17	60	SW Bailleul	Lines	5
6th	Ltn K Wolff	RE 8	9	Bois Bernard	GS	6
"	Ltn K Schäfer	BE 2	8	Givenchy	GS	10
"	Ltn K Schäfer	BE 2c	2	SW Vimy	GS	11
7th	Rittm M von Richthofen	Nieuport 17	60	NE Mercatel	Lines	37
"	Ltn K Wolff	Nieuport 17	60	"	Lines	7
"	Ltn K Schäfer	Nieuport 17	60	"	BrS	12
"	Vfw S Festner	Nieuport 23	60	Farbus	BrS	6
8th	Vfw S Festner	Nieuport 17	60	E Vimy	GS	7
"	Rittm M von Richthofen	Sopwith 2	43	Farbus	GS	38
"	Ltn K Wolff	DH 4	55	NE Blécourt	GS	8
"	Ltn K Schäfer	DH 4	55	Epinoy	GS	13
"	Rittm M von Richthofen	BE 2g	16	W Vimy	GS	39
9th	Ltn K Schäfer	BE 2d	4	Aix Noulette	BrS	14
11th	Vfw S Festner	BE 2d	13	N Monchy		8
"	Ltn K Schäfer	Bristol F 2a	48	SE Fresnes	GS	15
"	Ltn K Wolff	Bristol F 2a	48	N Fresnes	GS	9
"	Ltn L von Richthofen	Bristol F 2a	48	N Fresnes	GS	2
"	Rittm M von Richthofen	BE 2d	13	Willerval	GS	40
"	Ltn L von Richthofen	RE 8	59	NE Fampoux	BrS	3
"	Ltn K Schäfer	BE 2e	13	E Arras	BrS	16
13th	Vfw S Festner	RE 8	59	N Dury	GS	9
"	Ltn L von Richthofen	RE 8	59	NE Biache	GS	4
"	Ltn L von Richthofen	RE 8	59	Pelves	GS	5
"	Ltn K Wolff	RE 8	59	N Vitry	GS	10
"	Rittm M von Richthofen	RE 8	59	E Vitry	GS	41
"	Ltn K Wolff	FE 2b	11	S Bailleul	BrS	11
"	Rittm M von Richthofen	FE 2b	11	W Monchy	BrS	42
"	Ltn K Wolff	Nieuport 23	29	S Monchy	BrS	12
"	Ltn K Schäfer	FE 2b	11	SW Monchy	Lines	17
"	Ltn K Wolff	Martinsyde G 100	27	Rouvroy	GS	13
"	Vfw S Festner	FE 2b	25	E Harnes	GS	10
"	Rittm M von Richthofen	FE 2b	25	Noyelles-Godault	GS	4
14th	Rittm M von Richthofen	Nieuport 17	60	S Bois Bernard	GS	44
"	Ltn K Wolff	Nieuport 17	60	SE Drocourt	GS	14
"	Ltn L von Richthofen	Nieuport 17	60	E Fouquiéres	GS	6
"	Vfw S Festner	Nieuport 17	60	Gavrelle	Lines	11
"	Ltn K Schäfer	FE 2b	25	SE Lievin	BrS	18
"	Ltn K Schäfer	RE 8	34	SW Lieven	BrS	19
"	Ltn L von Richthofen	SPAD 7	19	SE Vimy	BrS	7
"	Ltn K Wolff	SPAD 7	19	W Bailleul	Lines	15
16th	Ltn L von Richthofen	Nieuport 17	60	S Roeux	Lines	8
"	Ltn K Wolff	Nieuport 17	60	NE Roeux	Lines	16
"	Vfw S Festner	Nieuport 17	60	NE Biache	GS	12
"	Rittm M von Richthofen	BE 2e	13	NW Gavrelle	BrS	45

Date	Pilot	Br type	Sqn	Location	G/B	Pilot's total
21st	Ltn L von Richthofen	Nieuport 17	29	SE Vimy	BrS	9
"	Ltn K Wolff	BE 2e	16	N Willerval	Lines	17
"	Ltn K Wolff	Nieuport 23	29	E Fresnes	GS	18
"	Ltn K Schäfer	Nieuport 17	29	Fresnes	Lines	20
22nd	Ltn K Wolff	FE 2b	11	Hendecourt	GS	19
"	Rittm M von Richthofen	FE 2b	11	Lagnicourt	BrS	46
"	Ltn K Wolff	Morane P	3	Havrincourt	Lines	20
"	Ltn K Schäfer	FE 2b	11	W Monchy	BrS	21
23rd	Rittm M von Richthofen	BE 2f	16	Méricourt	GS	47
"	Ltn L von Richthofen	BE 2g	16	N Vimy	BrS	10
25th	Ltn K Almenröder	RE 8	59	Guémappe	Lines	7
"	Ltn K Schäfer	FE 2b	25	N Bailleul	BrS	22
"	Ltn K Schäfer	Bristol F 2a	48	Bahnhoff Roeux	GS	23
26th	Ltn K Wolff	BE 2g	5	E Gavrelle	GS	21
"	Ltn L von Richthofen	BE 2c	16	SE Vimy Ridge	GS	11
"	Ltn K Allmenröder	BE 2g	16	Vimy Ridge	BrS	8
27th	Ltn L von Richthofen	FE 2b	11	Fresnes	GS	12
"	Ltn K Wolff	FE 2b	11	S Gavrelle	BrS	22
"	Ltn K Allmenröder	FE 2b	11	W Fampoux	BrS	9
28th	Rittm M von Richthofen	BE 2e	13	SE Pelves	GS	48
"	Ltn K Wolff	BE 2g	5	S Oppy	Lines	23
"	Ltn K Wolff	BE 2f	16	W Gavrelle	BrS	24
29th	Rittm M von Richthofen	SPAD 7	19	E Lécluse	GS	49
"	Ltn K Wolff	SPAD 7	19	Sailly	GS	25
"	Ltn L von Richthofen	SPAD 7	19	Izel	GS	13
"	Rittm M von Richthofen	FE 2b	18	SW Inchy	GS	50
"	Ltn K Wolff	FE 2b	18	S Pronville	BrS	26
"	Rittm M von Richthofen	BE 2e	12	Roeux	GS	51
"	Ltn L von Richthofen	BE 2e	12	NE Monchy	GS	14
"	Rittm M von Richthofen	Triplane	8N	N Hénin-Liétard	GS	52
30th	Ltn L von Richthofen	BE 2g	16	SE Vimy	Lines	15
"	Ltn L von Richthofen	FE 2d	57	Izel	GS	16
"	Ltn K Wolff	BE 2e	13	W Fresnes	BrS	27

Key

GS – German Side
BrS – British Side
Lines – frontline/trenches area

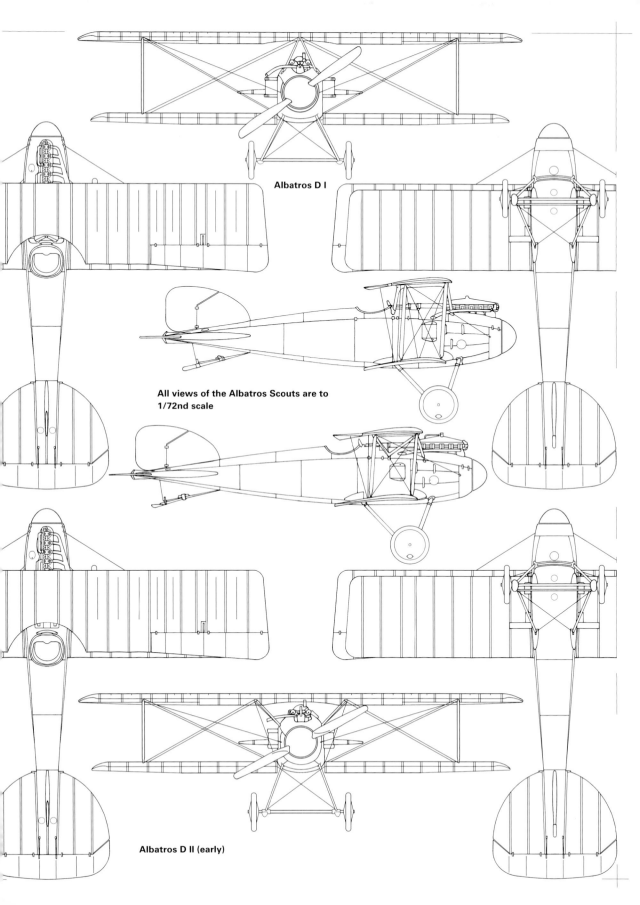

Albatros D I

All views of the Albatros Scouts are to
1/72nd scale

Albatros D II (early)

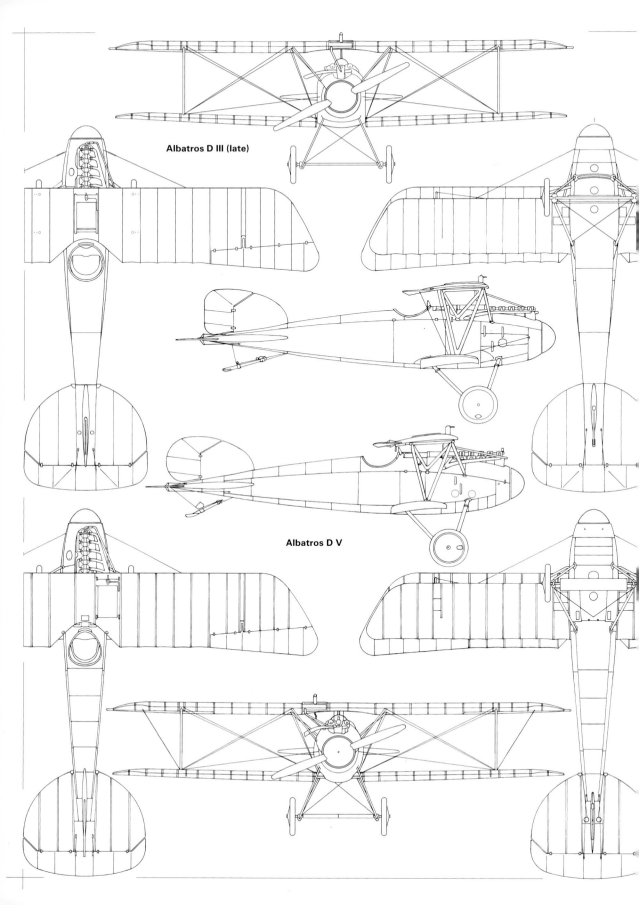

Albatros D III (late)

Albatros D V

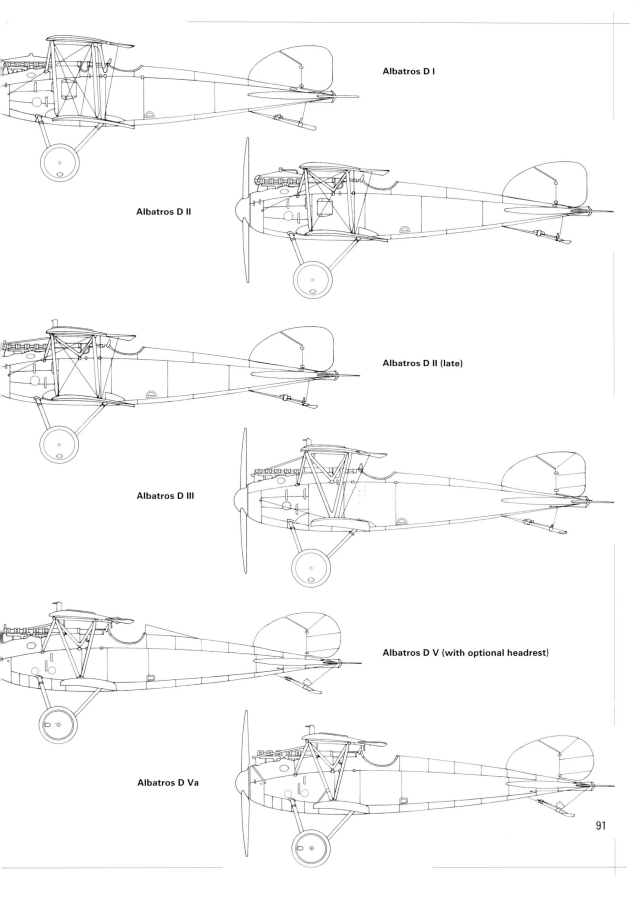

Albatros D I

Albatros D II

Albatros D II (late)

Albatros D III

Albatros D V (with optional headrest)

Albatros D Va

COLOUR PLATES

1

Albatros D II D.1724/16, flown by Ltn Karl Emil Schäfer, *Kasta* 11, early 1917

The early Albatros Scouts were attached to two-seater units just as the Fokker *Eindeckers* had been, and were grouped in a *Kampstaffel*, known as a *Kasta*. Many of the future aces flew in these units, including Schäfer, who was assigned to *Kasta* 11 (*Kampfgeschwader* 2). Unless painted in specific colours, the engine cowlings, spinners and struts of all Albatros Scouts were often grey. The plywood fuselage of this machine was lightly stained a reddish-brown, while the upper wing surfaces had early camouflage of dark green and chestnut (reddish) brown. Undersides were sky blue, whilst the rudder was left clear-doped fabric. The factory-finished national markings took the form of black crosses painted onto a white background, although many units overpainted much of the white area, leaving just a thin white edge (5 cm) to the cross – in this instance a lighter shade of brown has been used to overpaint the white area. In 1916 the fuselage and tail crosses initially remained on a white square background. Schäfer's personal markings consisted of white circles with a narrow black outline on both the fuselage sides and upper surfaces of the tailplane (see tailplane top view 1 for details). The wheel covers are also believed to have been white.

2

Albatros D II flown by Oblt Stephan Kirmaier, *Jasta* 2, 1916

After Oswald Boelcke's death in October 1916, Kirmaier took command of *Jasta* 2, where he flew this Albatros D II, which again has a reddish-brown stained plywood fuselage and top wing areas painted reddish-brown and dark green. Undersides and wheel covers were light blue, whilst the rudder was again left in clear-doped fabric. His personal marking was a narrow black band around the fuselage. Interestingly Kirmaier also had his groundcrew tie a black and white streamer between the wing struts to denote his position as *Staffelführer*.

3

Albatros D III flown by Ltn Hermann Frommherz of *Jasta* 2 Boelcke, 1917

Almost the whole aircraft, including upper and lower wing surfaces, was painted a light sky blue, with the exception of the tail area which was white aft of a thin black band round the rear fuselage. Struts and wheel covers were also pale blue. Finally, the D III bore a diagonal black and white band, edged in black and white, around the mid-fuselage section. Frommherz dubbed this aircraft *Blaue Maus* ('blue mouse'), and although he did not become an ace flying it, the D III's colouring is no less interesting, and its finish is immaculate.

4

Albatros D III flown by Gerhard Bassenge, *Jasta* 2, summer 1917

Gerhard Bassenge, like Frommherz, cut his combat teeth on the Albatros D III in the summer and autumn of 1917. By this time many Albatros Scouts had clear-varnished plywood fuselages, which gave them the yellow hue seen in these profiles.

Bassenge's machine had a grey nose, cowling, struts and wheel covers. The all-white tail marking of *Jasta* 2 is clear, as is the pilot's personal marking, which consists of a broad black fuselage band, edged in white, and a horizontal black and white stripe which runs from the engine to the fuselage band. Upper wing surfaces were dark green, light Brunswick green and reddish brown.

5

Albatros D III flown by Ltn Werner Voss, *Jasta* 2 Boelcke, mid-1917

Werner Voss, during his period with *Jasta* Boelcke, flew this much-decorated Albatros D III – he certainly used it in June 1917. While the cowling remained grey, the spinner was painted red and, of course, the empennage was finished in white aft of the thin black fuselage band of *Jasta* Boelcke. The 'yellow' colouring of the plywood fuselage was achieved through the application of varnish, onto which Voss had painted a red heart, edged white (repeated on the top decking) and a white swastika (a good luck symbol), surrounded by a green laurel wreath with a pale blue bow, again edged in white. Upper wing surfaces were pale Brunswick green, reddish-brown (Venetian) and dark olive green – not green and mauve, which came later. Often missed in drawings of this D III are two straight white bands mid-way, fore and aft, on the upper surface of the top wing (see wing planform 5 for details).

6

Albatros D III flown by Kurt Wüsthoff, *Jasta* 4, summer 1917

Wüsthoff flew an OAW-built Albatros D III adorned with the *Jasta* 4 unit marking of a black spiral band around the varnished ply fuselage. The machine also bears his personal marking, comprising a black tail with white rudder. The cowling and struts are all grey in colour, whilst the spinner is halved black and white. The upper surfaces of the wing are finished in green and mauve, with pale blue undersides, and the elevators also appear to be painted white.

7

Albatros D V flown by Uffz Paul Bäumer, *Jasta* 5, summer 1917

Bäumer flew this famously-marked Albatros D V in the summer of 1917. Both the nose spinner and a 10-cm band immediately behind it were painted red, and the cowling, struts and wheel covers were grey. The forward portion of the fuselage was left unpainted in varnished wood, whilst the rear fuselage from cockpit to tail were red, adorned with the pilot's personal Edelweiss marking. Finally, *Jasta* 5 had its own tail markings of green, edged in red. Bäumer's D V wore a large black *B* under each lower wing, these underwing surfaces being light sky blue (see wing underside planform 7 for details).

8

Albatros D V flown by Vfw Otto Könnecke, *Jasta* 5, 1917

Könnecke flew this green-painted D V, with red spinner and cowling and the tail in the same '*Jasta* 5 green' edged in red, as seen in the previous profile. Upper wing areas were also almost certainly green with a red chevron (see wing planform 8 for details), whilst the lower wing surfaces were painted light sky blue. However, the undersurfaces of the fuselage remained varnished plywood. Könnecke's personal insignia was a black and white chequerboard, edged in red.

9

Albatros D V flown by Vfw Fritz Rumey, *Jasta* 5, 1917

Fritz Rumey flew this uniquely-marked Albatros D V, which had its entire fuselage painted in candy-striping – to compliment the fuselage, the wing, cabane and wheel struts were also painted alternatively black and white, as were the wheel covers (port white and starboard black). The red nose and green tail, edged in red, again denote *Jasta* 5. The upper wing surfaces were green and mauve, and the undersurface areas light sky blue, with the letter *R* painted on the undersides of both lower wings (see wing underside planform 9 for details). To complete the complex markings on this uniquely decorated Albatros, Rumey had two white stripes applied to the tailplane and elevators (see tailplane top view 9 for details).

10

Albatros D V D.5284/17 flown by Vfw Josef Mai, *Jasta* 5, late 1917

Another famed ace with *Jasta* 5 was Josef Mai, who flew this distinctively-marked Albatros D Va from late 1917 through to early 1918. Its fuselage was varnished wood, but the upper decking had a mottled camouflage effect, thought to consist of light brown over dark green. The usual red spinner and cowling band, and green tail edged in red, denoted the *Jasta* markings, while his personal insignia was a black and white star and crescent, painted mid-way along the fuselage sides. Upper and lower mainplanes had five-colour lozenge fabric, while the struts and wheel covers were greyish-green in colour. Just visible attached to the fuselage, immediately forward of the wing strut, is an off-white coloured envelope in which the machine's rigging instructions were kept.

11

Albatros D V D.1148/17 flown by Ltn Hans Adam, *Jasta* 6, summer 1917

This D Va had the usual yellow varnish finish and a clear doped rudder and fin. The spinner appeared to be black, or at least dark grey, with a cowling band larger than that painted on *Jasta* 5 machines, although the cowling panels, struts and wheel covers remained in the standard grey colour. Adam's aircraft also boasted a large black fuselage band, edged in white, whilst the tailplane had black and white stripes top and bottom – the *Jasta* 6 identification marking (see tailplane top view 11 for details). Black and white stripes were also repeated on the lower wing undersides inboard of the national marking, and the wing tips were marked in black too (see wing underside planform 11 for details). Upper wing areas were mauve and green. Adam crashed this machine on 2 August 1917, although he emerged from the wreck unscathed.

12

Albatros D V flown by Ltn Josef Jacobs, *Jasta* 7, 1917

Black featured prominently on most of Josef Jacobs' aeroplanes in World War 1. This *Jasta* 7 Albatros D V was totally black except for upper and lower wing areas, which had five-colour lozenge fabric (see wing planform 12 for details). The national markings on the undersides of the lower wing were edged in white, and the aircraft also featured two additional

crosses smaller in size on the top wings. Jacobs' personal marking was two forward-slanting white fuselage bands positioned just aft of the cockpit. This machine has also been noted with a white, or at least clear-doped, rudder.

13

Albatros D V flown by Ltn Aloys Heldmann, *Jasta* 10, late 1917

Heldmann's machine was not dissimilar to Adam's scout in that it had a large dark (possibly black) fuselage band, edged in white, painted over its yellow varnished plywood. However, the tailplane was light blue in colour, and the D V also wore the yellow nose and cowling band of *Jasta* 10. Otherwise, the machine had standard factory-finish mauve and green upper wing surfaces and pale blue undersides, as well as a grey cowling, struts and wheel covers.

14

Albatros D III No 629/17 flown by Ltn Karl Allmenröder, *Jasta* 11, 1917

Much has been written about the red machines of *Jasta* 11, and indeed after von Richthofen took command he flew mainly red machines, although as 1917 progressed, his pilots too flew red-marked scouts, but each had a particular colour(s) to identify the pilot. For example, the D III flown by Allmen-röder had a red fuselage and tail, but with a white nose and elevator (see tailplane top view 14 for details). Also, its upper wing areas remained light Brunswick green, Venetian red (reddish-brown) and dark olive green, and the undersides pale blue.

15

Albatros D III flown by Ltn Lothar von Ricthofen, *Jasta* 11, early 1917

In the early days of 1917 before *Jasta* 11's all-red configuration became established, the red colour only covered small areas of the machine as seen in this profile. This D III was originally flown by Manfred von Richthofen, and it is widely believed that he downed several RFC machines in it. It was then passed onto his brother Lothar when he arrived on the *staffel*, and he also flew it as it shown here, with just a large red fuselage band aft of the cockpit. The rudder remained clear doped, whilst the spinner, cowling, wheel covers and struts were painted grey. Standard camouflage of olive green, Venetian red and light green covered the upper wing surfaces and tailplane, with the undersides being light blue.

16

Albatros D V flown by Ltn Carl-August von Schönebeck, *Jasta* 11, 1917

Von Schönebeck's early victories were scored in 1917 with *Jasta* 11, where he flew an Albatros D V that had had the whole of the forward fuselage area ahead of the cockpit painted red – including struts and wheel covers. The remainder of the fuselage was left yellow varnished, while the empennage was painted lilac as his personal marking. Upper and lower wing areas were covered in five-colour lozenge fabric.

17

Albatros D V flown by Ltn Ulrich Neckel, *Jasta* 12, 1917

Jasta 12's distinctive unit identification took the form of a black tail and rear fuselage, while many of its aircraft also fea-

tured white spinners with a black cowling band. Ulrich
Neckel's D V carried these markings, while his own personal
insignia was a white chevron with a black border painted
between the cockpit and the national marking. The rest of the
fuselage was varnished, although one panel forward of the
leading wing edge can be seen to be much darker – on this
was placed the envelope containing the rigging instructions.
The entire wing fabric was five-colour lozenge, with other
parts adorned in the usual grey paint. Finally, the wheel covers were either light grey or white.

18
Albatros D III flown by Oblt Rudolf Berthold, *Jasta* 14, April 1917

Rudolf Berthold's aircraft were noted for their winged sword
insignia. As CO of *Jasta* 14 in 1917, this marking appeared on
the yellow varnished fuselage of his D III around April. The
rudder was clear doped, while cowling, spinner, wheel covers
and struts were all grey. During this period the upper wing
surfaces were Brunswick green, light green and Venetian red.

19
Albatros D V flown by Ltn Kurt Monnington, *Jasta* 15, 1917

Kurt Monnington's D V wore this unusual scheme, the fuselage seemingly finished in a pale grey colour, or even silver-
grey, while the streaked camouflage was probably dark forest
green, which was also painted on the wheel covers, fin and
rudder. Upper wing areas were mauve and green, with light
blue undersides. His personal insignia was a skull and crossbones white and ivory in colour, with grey and black detailing.

20
Albatros D V flown by Oliver Frhr von Beaulieu-Marconnay, *Jasta* 15, 1917

Jasta 15 eventually settled on red and Prussian blue identification colours, and these were made famous by Berthold and
his pilots. Each machine was painted in these colours – red
from spinner to the end of the engine cowling, and blue from
this point aft, leaving just the undersides, wheel struts and
covers in pale blue. The wing and cabane struts were also
believed to be red in colour. The national marking on the fuselage sides was also overpainted. Upper wing surfaces were
generally mauve and green. Each pilot had his own personal
insignia, von Beaulieu-Marconnay's being a merged 4D.
'branding iron', denoting his former 4th Dragoon Regiment.

21
Albatros D V flown by Ltn Georg von Hantelmann, *Jasta* 15, early 1918

Marked in the *Jasta* 15 colours of blue and red, the cabane
struts, wheel covers and wheel struts were also painted in
the latter colour, while the interplane struts were grey. The
rudder, like the wing and horizontal tailplane, was covered in
five-colour lozenge fabric. Von Hantelmann's personal
emblem was the skull and crossbones, in white and black.

22
Albatros D II flown by Ltn Ludwig Hanstein, *Jasta* 16b, 1916-17

The Bavarian *Jasta* 16b had several successful pilots, one of

whom was Ludwig Hanstein. In his early career with this unit
he flew this Albatros D II, its plywood fuselage being stained
a reddish-brown and the rudder remaining clear doped. Wing
upper surfaces were painted in dark green and chestnut
brown camouflage, with light blue undersides. Unlike other
machines in the unit, this D II carried upper wing crosses on
white squares. Hanstein's personal insignia was a white vertical rectangle on which appeared three small vertical squares,
and these may have been dark blue (Bavarian) in colour,
although with the pilot being a Prussian, they were probably
black. Hanstein survived a collision in this machine, although
the Albatros was wrecked in the incident.

23
Albatros D V flown by Ltn Theodor Rumpel, *Jasta* 16b, 1917

Entirely decorated in personal markings, Rumpel's D V had a
black forward area from its spinner to the rear of its engine
cowling, followed by zebra-striping back to the tail, which
included the forward section of the fin. What remained of the
fin was varnished plywood, while the rudder was clear doped.
Struts and wheel covers were grey, and the upper wing surfaces were mauve and green, with light sky blue undersides.

24
Albatros D V flown by Ltn Otto Kissenberth, *Jasta* 16b, mid-1917

Kissenberth flew this all-black fuselage D V, which had just its
rudder left unpainted in clear-doped fabric. Wing upper surfaces were standard mauve and green, with light sky blue
undersides, and the struts and wheel covers were grey. His
personal emblem was a while edelweiss alpine flower, out-
lined in black and with yellow stamens. This marking took a
slightly different form on the opposite side of the fuselage.

25
Albatros D III D.1072/16 flown by Ltn Josef Jacobs, *Jasta* 22, spring 1917

Prior to his long service with *Jasta* 7, Josef Jacobs had
enjoyed some success flying with *Jasta* 22 in the first half of
1917. Although subsequently to fly predominantly all-black
machines, he used this reddish-brown stained D III in the
spring of 1917. Its upper wing areas and tailplane were painted in dark green and a darker chestnut brown, with the latter
colouring also being used to mark the rudder. Undersides of
all wings were light sky blue, as were the wheel covers,
whilst the nose cowling and struts were uniform grey.
Jacobs' personal markings included a three-pointed Mercedes
star, edged in white, with a white circle in the middle. He was
usually known as 'Kobes', which was written in black on a
white background on the fuselage. This particular D III was an
LVG-built machine.

26
Albatros D V D.2263/17 flown by Otto Kissenberth, *Jasta* 23b, summer 1917.

After service with *Jasta* 16b, Otto Kissenberth was made
leader of *Jasta* 23b, where he again flew an all-black Albatros
D V, although on this occasion its wing struts were grey. The
aircraft also featured his personal white and yellow edelweiss
fuselage marking, and all wing surfaces were covered in five-

colour lozenge fabric. The serial number was painted in white on the fin, although the '/17' was omitted.

27
Albatros D V flown by Ltn Friedrich Ritter von Röth, *Jasta* 23b in early 1918.

Fritz von Röth was the top-scoring 'balloon-buster' in the German Air Service. His Albatros D V was finished in yellow varnished plywood, with all metal cowling panels, wheel covers and struts being painted grey and the spinner white. All wing areas were covered in five-colour lozenge fabric. Personal marking consisted of a black and white circle on the fuselage below and aft of the cockpit, which partially covered the aircraft's weight details, and von Röth also had a white band encircling the rudder and tailplane (the *Jasta* marking). The central area of the tail was also painted white, back to the elevator (see wing planform 27 for details). As an OAW-built D V, the plaquettes denoting its place of manufacture were located just beneath the cockpit rim. Although not visible on the profile, printed on the V-strut was the letter 'L' above the D V's serial number, and above this was 'A.W.S. D.5a.', with '(O.A.W.)' underneath – the former stood for *Albatros Werke Schneidemühl* and the latter *Ostdeutsch Albatros Werke*.

28
Albatros D V D.2214/17 flown by Ltn Heinrich Kroll, *Jasta* 24, summer 1917

This machine is believed to have had standard factory-finish varnished ply sides, mauve and green upper wing areas and blue undersides. The rudder remained clear-doped, while standard grey was applied to all metal panels and the nose cone, as well as the wheel covers. The struts were also grey in colour, and on the leading edge of the starboard one could be seen the letter 'R' (for right), while the serial number was also marked on the rear V-strut. Kroll's personal marking of a black and white 'Yin-Yang' symbol was worn on both fuselage sides, and was repeated not only on the top decking but also on the fuselage underside.

29
Albatros D V D.2299/17 flown by Oblt Bruno Loerzer, leader of *Jasta* 26, autumn 1917

In most *Jasta* stores black and white paint tended to be the most common colours to be found, so it is not surprising that many aircraft were decorated in these shades which, of course, gave them a Germanic 'feel'. Loerzer chose to have alternate black and white bands painted around the whole fuselage of his D V, along with a totally black tailplane – with the exception of a white band that ran spanwise across the tail, which formed the unit marking for *Jasta* 26. Wing areas were covered in five-colour lozenge fabric and the wheel covers were grey. Cabane struts were probably painted black and the V-struts grey. Continuing the black and white theme was Loerzer's personal six-pointed star on the fuselage. The serial number remained visible on the fin, painted onto varnished wood, although the '/17' portion of it had been obliterated.

30
Albatros D III flown by Ltn Hermann Göring, leader of *Jasta* 27, June 1917

A close friend of Bruno Loerzer, Hermann Göring flew with

him in *Jasta* 26 before becoming leader of *Jasta* 27 in mid-1917. Göring used this Albatros D III during his early period with his new unit, and again black and white predominated – an all black fuselage, with white spinner, tailplane and struts. Its upper wing surfaces were light Brunswick green, dark olive green and Venetian red, with the wing undersides being painted in light blue. As leader, Göring also carried two inverted white bands on the upper wing surface and a single black inverted band on the underside of the lower wing, together with the number '1' on each (see wing and underside planforms 30 for details). He had earlier flown this machine in *Jasta* 26, where it had worn different markings, and had duly taken it with him on 21 May 1917 to his new command. The D III was written off on 16 July.

31
Albatros D III D.774/17 flown by Oblt Otto Hartmann, leader of *Jasta* 28, 1917

This aircraft had a varnished plywood fuselage, while its rudder was clear yellowish dope, lighter than the fuselage. Spinner and cowling panels were standard grey, as were the struts and wheel covers. Hartmann's personal marking was a broad dark (probably red) fuselage band mid-way along the fuselage. Upper wing surfaces were painted in the three-tone camouflage, with pale blue undersides.

32
Albatros D III D.2090/17 flown by Vfw Fritz Jacobson, *Jasta* 31, April 1917

Yet another Albatros with a clear-varnished plywood fuselage and tail with clear-doped fabric rudder, as well as a standard grey spinner, cowling panels, struts and wheel covers. Upper wing areas were painted in light Brunswick green, dark olive green and Venetian red, with the undersurfaces finished in light sky blue. Jacobson's personal insignia was a band of black and white diamonds, edged in white. Note the unusual metal faring over machine gun breeches and high windshield. As with many other aircraft from *Jasta* 31, this machine later had camouflage mottling applied over its entire fuselage.

33
Albatros D V flown by Ltn Robert Greim, *Jasta* 34b, late 1917 through to early 1918

Whole fuselage and tail painted a whitish-silver (aluminium, with some white pigment added), which was the *Jasta* marking. This also extended to all struts and wheel covers, although the V-struts may have remained grey. Greim's personal markings comprised a red spinner and two large red fuselage bands just aft of the cockpit. Upper wing surfaces were mauve and green and undersides pale sky blue.

34
Albatros D V D.4483/17 flown by Ltn August Delling, *Jasta* 34b, spring 1918

Delling also flew with *Jasta* 34b, and his Albatros D V also had the whitish-silver fuselage colouring. The whole of the nose and forward fuselage back to the cockpit was painted a reddish-orange, with a similarly-coloured broad fuselage band appearing aft of the cockpit – Delling had a small cockade marking denoting a bullet hit (and dated '4 IV 18') painted in the middle of the fuselage band. The aircraft's rudder was finished in white, while the upper surfaces of the horizontal tail were standard mauve and green (see tailplane top view 34 for details) and the undersides pale blue. The wing areas were covered in five-colour lozenge fabric.

35

Albatros D V D.2284/17 flown by Ltn Hans Waldhausen, *Jasta* 37, late summer 1917

Waldhausen flew this well known D V during his brief career with this unit, all six of his kills being scored in the fighter over a period of just nine days. Half of his tally was claimed on his final flight, which ended when he in turn was brought down. The Albatros had a standard natural varnished ply fuselage and tail, with grey cowling panels and struts. The *Jasta* markings from this period included the black spinner and black and white wheel covers. Wing areas and the rudder (which also boasted an Albatros logo) were covered with five-colour lozenge fabric, while the tail surfaces were painted in diagonal black/white stripes, which also denoted *Jasta* 37 (see tailplane top view 35 for details). Waldhausen's personal marking took the form of a black and white star and crescent painted on the fuselage, the star repeated on the top decking.

36

Albatros D Va flown by Ltn Ernst Udet, leader of *Jasta* 37, late 1917

Ernst Udet is well known for his *LO*-marked Fokker D VII, but not so well known is his similarly-painted Albatros D Va, which he flew with *Jasta* 37 in the winter of 1917-18. The machine was totally black except for the lozenge fabric wing surfaces and *Jasta* 37 tail striping (see tailplane top view 36 for details). His personal *LO* emblem was painted in white, as was the 'V', or arrow head, marking on the nose area. Typical of aircraft assigned to *Jasta* leaders, Udet's fighter featured two white bands mid-way across both upper wings, and a large white *U* on the port lower wing undersides (see wing and underside planforms 36 for details). His machine also carried two black and white streamers attached to the elevators.

37

Albatros D Va flown by Ltn Helmut Dilthey, leader of *Jasta* 40s, mid-1918

As leader of *Jasta* 40s, Helmut Dilthey flew this Albatros D Va with its distinctive Saxon colours of light green and white fuselage bands, which extended to the tailplane (see tailplane top view 37 for details). Upper wing areas were covered in lozenge fabric, but the square area beneath the national marking was also pale green (see wing planform 37 for details). Wheel covers were also green, but the struts were the standard grey colour. Note the fuselage cross is further forward than normal. Dilthey may have been flying this aircraft when he was killed in action on 9 July 1918.

38

Albatros D III flown by Ltn Franz Ray, *Jasta* 49, 1918

Ray flew this OAW-built Albatros D III – OAW D IIIs all had rounded rudders similar to the D V. The fighter's fuselage was painted all black, including the spinner and cowling panels, but with a white fin and rudder. Upper wing areas were covered in five-colour lozenge fabric, and the wing crosses on both the upper and lower surfaces had white edges. The

tailplane's surfaces were black with two white stripes (see tailplane top view 38 for details).

39

Albatros D III D.2385/17 flown by Ltn Paul Strähle, *Staffelführer* of *Jasta* 57, spring 1918

Strähle flew this OAW-built Albatros D III whilst serving as *Staffelfhrer* of *Jasta* 57. As this profile shows, unit markings consisted of a pale blue fuselage, with the pilot in turn choosing to have the fighter's spinner, forward fuselage and wheel covers painted red, and the fin and rudder rendered in white. All wing areas were covered in five-colour lozenge fabric, while all struts were painted grey. Strähle's deputy leader in early 1918 was Hans Viebig, and he flew a similarly-marked Albatros, except that his personal colour was orange and the fighter lacked a white tail.

40

Albatros D V D.2092/17 flown by Ltn Walter B'ning, *Staffelführer* of *Jasta* 76b, early 1918

This machine may have also been flown by Böning during his earlier period with *Jasta* 19. It had a natural varnished plywood fuselage and tail, but with a cobalt (Bavarian) blue rudder. Spinner and nose band were also in white, with a second band in the same blue. Struts, cowling and wheel covers were in grey, whilst the upper wing area was mauve and green, with light sky blue undersurfaces. The D V's tailplane may have also been painted cobalt blue, with two white stripes, which was the marking of *Jasta* 76b (see tailplane top view 40 for details). Böning's personal marking was a black *B* on a white fuselage band, which was edged in black.

41

Albatros D Va flown by Eduard Ritter von Schleich, JGr 8, spring 1918

As with von Schleich's other aircraft, this machine was painted all-black, including all the struts, spinner and engine cowling panels. A white edelweiss had originally been worn on the fuselage just aft of the cockpit, but this too had been overpainted, although it was just visible. All wing areas were covered in five-colour lozenge fabric (see wing planform 41 for details). Known as the 'Black Knight', von Schleich had flown a near-identical Albatros D V when with *Jasta* 23b, although the latter aircraft had a white spinner.

42

Albatros D Va D.5815/18 flown by Gerhard Hubrich, *Seefrosta* 1, summer 1918

This aircraft had its varnished plywood finish camouflaged in a mottled effect using olive green paint applied more heavily to the top of the fuselage. All Marine fighter units employed chrome yellow as the unit identification colour, and Hubrich's machine boasted a 'warm' chrome yellow spinner and nose band – this same colour was applied to the tail, with the exception of a white rudder. Upper wing areas were mauve and green and undersides light sky blue. Note that the fuselage cross had also been slightly overpainted. Flugmeister Hubrich's personal insignia was a yellow chick with a red beak, emerging from a white egg, all of which was painted onto a dark blue panel. This referred to his nickname of *Küchen* ('chicken').